THE
FAMILY
NEST
EGG

THE
FAMILY
NEST
EGG

The Complete and Proven Financial Guide to Building Long-Term Wealth and Security

LAURA MEIER

AUTHOR OF

GOOD PARENTS WORRY, GREAT PARENTS PLAN

DIVERSION
BOOKS

For more information, email info@diversionbooks.com

Diversion Books
A division of Diversion Publishing Corp.
www.diversionbooks.com

First Diversion Books edition, January 2021
Paperback ISBN: 9781635767483
eBook ISBN: 9781635767490

Printed in The United States of America

1 3 5 7 9 10 8 6 4 2

Library of Congress cataloging-in-publication data is available on file

This book is dedicated to my parents, Allen and Christine King. Thank you for being incredible role models for me, Ben, Sara, Kelly, and Will, and teaching us what really matters most in life—faith, family, service, and of course, warm homemade chocolate chip cookies.

CONTENTS

INTRODUCTION

YEARS AGO, I SAT AT a small, seaside gathering with my whole life ahead of me. I was in my senior year of college with big plans to go to law school, start a successful career, get married, have a family, make great money, and accomplish big things.

As I sat there listening to the speaker's message that morning, I soon found she had a much more realistic take on what life would bring. She spoke of how the storms in life would come, and she asked her listeners how we'd get through them and how we'd be prepared.

I remember hoping I wouldn't have such storms in my life. *I want to be like that woman in the J. Crew catalog, with her family looking posh in their khakis and the grand white walls and rustic beams behind them. They're not freaking out about their bank account balances or having to change careers.*

Fast forward years later and here I am—here we all are now—with our rising rents and mortgages, kids, careers, and financial obligations, all caught together in the most unexpected storm of the century, a storm of such magnitude that it brought the entire world to a screeching halt and transformed our daily lives.

COVID-19 hit, and it hit HARD.

One morning we were rushing out the door in work clothes to drop the kids at school, and the next sheltered at home in total shock and sweatpants, trying to help the kids log onto Zoom.

Our conversations changed from who was driving the kids to practice today to those bigger questions we had been putting off when life was so bustling and busy: *How will we get through this? Is my family prepared?*

The truth is that most of us were not.

Before COVID-19 even hit:

- 89 percent of us had debt;
- 77 percent of us did not have at least six months' worth of living expenses saved in an emergency fund for a crisis;[1]
- 70 percent of us did not have our will or trust set up, or a legal document designating guardians to raise our kids if something happened to us;[2]
- 50 percent of us did not have any money saved for retirement.[3]

And, may I add, 100 percent of us were not prepared for homeschool.

Too many of us did not have our finances in order nor the protections we needed in place—not for this pandemic, nor for any other misfortunes or challenges in life we hoped would somehow magically skip our family, like someone losing their job, someone walking out, someone getting sick, or even worse, someone (even ourselves) passing away.

Too many of us were not financially prepared for the good things in life either, like buying a family home in the neighborhood where we want to live, maximizing our money so we can work less and earn more, or realizing a personal dream like starting our own business, taking a dream vacation or retiring early. Important life milestones were merely hopes rather than plans.

And we knew this. We knew we should stop sending our financial advisor to voicemail or skipping those 401(k) lunch-and-learns.

We knew we should put together a game plan to help finance the future we wanted. But it wasn't because we were being bad parents or giving up that we didn't have these plans in place; we were just busy, overwhelmed, and unsure how to tackle such daunting tasks. Between work demands, carpools, soccer games, and housework, we, regrettably, did not make building our wealth and securing our future the priority it needed to be.

Many of us also felt demotivated. It's not easy buying a family home where we want to live when housing prices are through the roof. It's not easy starting our own business or changing companies when the economy is volatile. It's not easy saving for our kids' colleges when we still have our own student loans to pay off. It's not easy saving for retirement when there's a million other pressing financial needs we have to deal with right now. And we're definitely not comfortable thinking of the "what if's" in life, like: what would happen to our family and finances if something happened to us?

And for all of us happily married couples out there, well, it is not always easy getting in sync and making these decisions with our spouse.

So putting things off just seemed easier.

But let's be honest. We know now that we don't have that luxury. Life is happening and it has its unexpected ups and downs. We saw what happened to a lot of families during COVID-19— families who lost their jobs, families who had someone get sick, and families who did not have the basic finances or protections in place to get through even a week of furlough.

For those of us who were not severely affected by COVID-19, we know we dodged a bullet that could have easily taken us down because we know we were not prepared.

Are we going to be the parents who must move our family out of our home because we got furloughed?

Are we going to be the parents whose finances will tank if the stock market dips?

Are we going to be the parents who can't eventually retire because we got wiped out during our working years?

Are we going to be the parents who end up on the GoFundMe page because something bad happened and we didn't have the financial resources or proper insurance in place?

I don't know about you, but I don't want to be a statistic. I want to be the other guy!

We all want the best for our families, especially our kids. We spend most of our everyday life just trying to make theirs better and happier. We want to wake up knowing that we are in control of our finances, rather than our finances being in control of us. We want to hit all those important life milestones, like buying a home, taking our dream trip, or funding our kids' colleges without having to worry about money. And we don't want to just grind it out in life, we want to have a purpose and achieve our family and personal dreams. And we definitely want to make sure our family and kids are totally protected if, God forbid, anything unexpected should happen to us.

We want to know how to build wealth and secure our family's future, and we want to do it as soon as possible.

And that is exactly what this book is all about!

Through how-to steps and inspiring real-life stories of everyday families, I will show you how the Three Ps for Prosperity—Plan, Protect, and Players—will help your family build wealth and secure your family's future, no matter what life may bring.

Together we are going to understand:

- The easy **If Life Were Perfect** technique that will help you stop basing your everyday financial decisions on your circumstances or limitations, and instead on what you really want in life.

- The easy P.E.A.C.E. process for taking control of your family's finances and getting in agreement with your spouse over money.
- How to build wealth while still having the time, flexibility, and lifestyle you want.
- How to stop worrying about the what-ifs in life and instead have peace of mind, knowing that your family would be completely taken care of if anything should happen to you.
- How to build your dream team of players who can help you reach financial milestones and achieve family goals.

Plus, I've included the easy 21-Day Family Nest Egg Plan to help your family get started and knock it out of the park!

Now, I am not as naïve as I was back at that gathering when I was twenty-one. As an estate planning attorney and parent of four growing (and expensive) kids, I am fully aware of the financial challenges that our families face. I know that life is not always easy, and yes, some of you really do, unfairly, have it way harder than others. But with the right approach and the right guidance, we can take control of our finances, prosper, plan for the people we love, and protect them no matter what life may bring.

And as for that speaker, well, she was right. Life's storms will erupt. They may not always come in the form of a major pandemic or the unfair personal challenges we have at hand, but they will continue to come in their own unique and unexpected ways.

You can get through them, and you can be prepared.

And I believe *you can come out even stronger.*

I want your family to be a success story, and I know you do, too. I am in this with you here and now, to help you get on the right financial track for your family. This is your time. This is your new opportunity to build your family nest egg and financially become the family you wish to be!

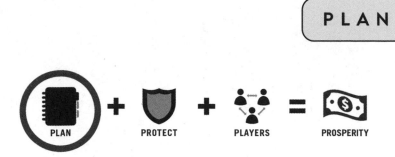

PLAN + PROTECT + PLAYERS = PROSPERITY

1

IF LIFE WERE PERFECT

PRAVIN WAS A YOUNG MAN WITH no more than a hundred dollars in his pocket when he immigrated to the US. His parents, who raised him and his ten siblings in a tiny flat in India, borrowed the money for his plane ticket here. Pravin enrolled in college and worked several jobs to support himself. Upon graduating, he returned to India, met his wife Sudha through an arranged marriage, and together they returned to America with little waiting for them here.

But together they had a vision of what their life could become.

Pravin and Sudha's love grew deeply. She provided him a strong foundation for his ambition and will, and he quickly climbed the corporate ladder, working his way into management. Meanwhile, Sudha gave birth to their two children and learned English, the only language her husband would speak to her in. Pravin invested in diversified ventures, and eventually cashed out shares he had acquired from his job as a general manager of a large company to fund his own. Somewhere in there he even went back to school part-time to earn his MBA.

Eventually, Pravin turned his business into a multi-million-dollar enterprise, which their daughter and son-in-law run together today. Their son became a highly regarded pediatric emergency room physician in Los Angeles. The family was incredibly close, and Pravin and Sudha were over the moon to become grandparents. They never forgot where they came from, either, as they would regularly send money back to their homeland to help their family and build up the community. They funded the Pratham Mody Technical Institute, a mega campus of Pratham—an innovative learning organization created to improve the quality of education across India.

If you think Pravin and Sudha's success was just luck, you're wrong. When he sought my assistance for legal planning to help him pass on his assets and preserve his legacy when the time came, Pravin told me that he and his wife's *vision* of what their life could become, along with smart financial choices, were the reasons for their success—their family, their wealth, and their legacy.

Pravin passed away a couple of years ago. If he were here with us today, he would tell us to have a vision for our future, manage our finances well, and believe all things are possible.

Like Pravin and Sudha, and countless other families who have stepped outside of their limiting circumstances to pursue a better life, we too need a vision for what our family, our finances, and our future can become.

We also know that such vision is not easy to develop when we are overwhelmed with raising a family, trying to make a good income, and dealing with life's everyday problems.

Most of the parents I meet tell me that planning for a better future seems daunting at best. As a parent myself, I totally get it!

But I want to change all that for you right now. Planning for your finances, your family, and your future is not another impossible box you're supposed to check, or another unmanageable task you need to complete. I want you to feel that same excitement about this journey that Pravin and Sudha likely felt, as you start thinking about creating the life you want for your family—a life beyond your current limitations.

To help you identify what that life looks like, I want you to consider these questions I will ask. When you think of your answers, don't think about what's realistic or possible or doable right now. Think about what you really want instead. Just think. Aloud or in your head. Don't record your answers in any way yet. Are you ready?

What if life were perfect?

Where would you be living, what would you be doing, and who would you surround yourself with?

Imagine that you really could become who you were meant to be...

Did you take some time to dream? Good. Hold on to it. We'll give it form shortly.

While we all know that life can never truly be perfect, too many of our families sell ourselves short and lack a vision for our lives. We let our finances and circumstances control us and limit us from reaching our full potential. Having a vision of how we want our life to be is where a family's transformation begins.

My husband and I can relate to anyone who feels visionless, and we've discussed it on our podcast, *If Life Were Perfect.* Back in 2010, when our kids were small and I had another one on the way, our family vision was basically to survive the day and hope life would magically get easier. We were both working at major law firms, overwhelmed by the cost of living in a super expensive city, shelling out money for babysitting and preschools, renting from a landlord I still don't like to this day, and fighting with each other because there was so much to do and we were both pointing fingers at each other. That's when we said, enough is enough, and knew something had to change.

That is when we took a step back and asked ourselves to do what I'm asking you to do—we popped the question, "What if life were perfect?" and instantly felt like our entire future opened up to us again.

Asking—and answering—that question helped us create a whole new vision for our future. We ended up saying goodbye to those big law firm jobs and started our own law firm from our kitchen table, even smack dab in the middle of a recession. It grew to become one of the premier estate planning law firms in California, and we expanded with additional businesses in the finance space as well. Now, we not only help guide families who are our clients, but we also help others through our *If Life Were Perfect* podcast, which made it on Apple Podcast's *New and Noteworthy* and *Top Shows* (woohoo!), through workshops conducted for parents at cool places like Fortune 500 companies, and through appearances on television news and other major media outlets.

We said goodbye to the landlord a few years ago and bought the family home we wanted and in the neighborhood we wanted. We have the time and flexibility to raise our kids and be there to really enjoy them. We got to travel a lot before COVID-19, and enjoy regular day dates and time for ourselves to do what we want to do. And we get to help lift our community through serving on local charity boards and through our faith practice.

While our life is not exactly *perfect*, and we've had our ups and downs along the way, as every family will, we are living the life we envisioned back in 2010 when we were drowning in our circumstances and decided to make a change. We know firsthand what a game changer a vision can be.

I want you to have that **If Life Were Perfect** vision for your family so I can help you create a plan to get there.

There's a simple, easy trick you can do right now that will get you 43 percent closer to reaching that **If Life Were Perfect** vision you have in your mind.

Dr. Gail Matthews, a psychology professor at the Dominican University in California, researched the art and science of goal setting and discovered that, just by writing down your goals on paper, you can get 43 percent closer to reaching them.

If I could get 43 percent closer to having more money, to taking more trips, to not fighting so much with my husband, and to preparing for an early retirement just by writing it down, I'd have a pen and paper on hand all day long!

I want to show you how this technique of writing down our goals worked for us in real life when my husband and I were trying to find the right home to buy for our family. We were having trouble finding something that was a) big enough for our family, b) in the city where we were renting, and c) within our price range. I had spent countless hours on Zillow and just wasn't finding anything we wanted.

That's when we took out a pen and paper and wrote down in an **If Life Were Perfect** list all the things we ideally wanted in a home. We wrote down our ideal neighborhood vibe, proximity to work, school rankings, number of bedrooms, square footage, safety, and so on. Although affordability was a real issue for us, we set that aside for a moment and pretended it did not matter. All options were on the table so we could be honest about what we really wanted.

After we made the list and could physically see in writing what we were looking for, we had much more clarity and realized the neighborhood we wanted most to live in was our current one, and not the more expensive areas in town. We also realized that a home a few streets over that we had previously toured and dismissed matched the criteria on our **If Life Were Perfect** list. With a little price negotiation, we bought it, and are so happy living here. Had we not gone through that process and written down our goals and what we wanted most, we could have easily overlooked what turned out to be the perfect home for us.

Making an **If Life Were Perfect** list for those big goals you want to reach in life (like retiring at a certain age), or those milestones you want to reach (like buying a family home), will be the game changer for you to get what you ultimately want. Having this list will become your new GPS to guide you and remind you where you want to go, and help you to not get sidetracked or give up along the way.

So now, it's your turn. Take the dreaming you did in the previous section and apply it to this **If Life Were Perfect** Worksheet. Write. It. Down. And keep it with you as move through this book. You get to decide now what you want most and watch those new doors begin to open.

IF LIFE WERE PERFECT
A WORKSHEET

Think of your answers to these questions, not about what is practical today, but ultimately what you want most:

If life were perfect...

I would spend my days with these people:

These current problems would be gone:

These debts would be gone:

I would have this level of education, knowledge, or skill:

I would do this for my job or start my own business that does this:

I would personally accomplish these things:

I would have money growing for me without my own efforts through these types of investments:

I would buy a home in this neighborhood:

I would pay for my children to attend this type of college:

I would travel to these places:

I would have money to pay for these special life events:

I would have the option to retire by this age and have this type of lifestyle:

I would help with or donate to these organizations or causes:

I would leave behind this legacy:

I also want to include this in my **If Life Were Perfect** vision:

Now that we know where you are headed, I'm going to help you put together a family nest egg plan to get you there using the Three Ps for Prosperity—Plan, Protect, and Players. I'll include advice from other financial professionals, like a financial advisor, CPA, mortgage lender, and others, as your family nest egg plan will require many areas of expertise. I'm used to quarterbacking this whole process for my clients, so I will make sure you are getting all the information you need!

And here's a final warning before we get planning, because too many families identify what they want, only to slip back into their old ways or settle for what's at hand. I need you to tell yourself that no matter what changes you need to make, no matter the bumps that will come along the way, and no matter how rocky the road may be, that you are going to approach your journey with a winning attitude. No. Matter. What.

If you are a sports fan, you might remember the AFC championship game in 2019 between the Patriots and the Chiefs that determined who would go on to play in the Super Bowl. (Don't worry, you don't have to like Tom Brady to like this story!) I was at a party when I heard a lot of commotion coming from the living room, and our friends were yelling that the Patriots just gave up the game. I saw that the Chiefs had pulled ahead with little time left in the game, and that Brady was not happy. I had never really watched the Patriots play before and had not been watching the game, but I saw Brady get off the bench and get back in the game, even though it looked like his chances of winning were shot. But you would have never known that from watching him and his offense. In fact, they took the field and Brady lasered the ball, play after play, down the field toward the endzone, like a robotic terminator. I thought, I don't know how they'll pull this off, but these guys aren't going to let themselves lose. They're playing to win. And you know what? They did. And they also went on to win the Super Bowl that year (much to my son's dismay).

That's the winning attitude we all need if we are going to achieve those things on our **If Life Were Perfect** list. We must believe that, regardless of the clock, the score, the obstacles, the fears, or what's happened in the past, we can go after our **If Life Were Perfect** list and win.

It's time to put on your helmet, it's time to storm the field, and it's time to be in it to win it. Now let's get planning!

2

BUDGETING

IF YOU ARE GOING TO achieve all those things on your **If Life Were Perfect** list, you are going to need to create a financial plan to get there. Because if you are not in control of your finances, then you are not in control of your future!

And the first leg of your journey begins with setting up a budget.

Now, I want you to be totally honest: What comes to your mind when you think of the word budget?

While technically a budget is defined as an estimation of revenue and expenses over a set time period, most of us define a budget as "no fun" or "ball and chain" or "tight leash."

And that's partially why we end up with those statistics showing how most of us parents do not have the financial resources we should for our future, or why there are people out there with money who are still not achieving their **If Life Were Perfect** vision.

If you ask most people whether they want to go on a budget, they will tell you no thanks. It sounds about as much fun as going on a diet or a trip to the dentist.

But I want to change that for you.

I want you to hear the word budget and think, "amazing" and "freeing" and "dream maker." If I can accomplish that by the end of this chapter, you owe me a latte! That's because having a budget is less about giving things up, and more about getting what you really want—those things on your **If Life Were Perfect** list.

It's about using your money to support your efforts to solve your problems or reach your goals, rather than being limited by your finances.

It's about being honest with yourself (and others) about what you can afford.

It's about managing your finances based on the numbers, and not on feelings or impulses.

And it's about laying a firm foundation for building your family wealth.

The question is not whether you need a budget, but whether you have the courage to make one.

A BUDGET IS FOR EVERYONE

Most of us think budgets are for people who are struggling to make ends meet, or people who are not spontaneous or fun. But really, a budget is for all of us who are serious about getting the life we want for our family and having the wisdom and discipline to maximize our hard-earned dollars to get there.

I can't tell you how many families I work with who make fantastic incomes, yet when I look at their overall finances, they are falling short of securing their family's future and reaching all their goals. Just because we make money does not mean we are managing it wisely or building it to help us get where we want to be.

I think of my client who was married to a famous athlete. You would know his name. He made millions of dollars during his career and spent every last penny of it. Now, while most of us are not making that kind of money, how many of us are spending so much that it's costing us our hopes and plans for our futures?

How do you see a budget as helping your family right now?

Are you the family who earns tons of money but is still not setting aside enough for retirement?

Are you the family who makes a modest living and feels guilty about spending money on a trip?

Are you the family who is struggling with debt and feels like you cannot seem to get ahead?

Whatever category you see yourself in, a budget is the change you need. It's the foundation for building wealth and securing your family's future. It is the only way to ensure that every dollar you make is being maximized to get you what you ultimately want— what you identified on your **If Life Were Perfect** list!

MY BUDGETING JOURNEY

I used to think of a budget in the traditional sense, where you cut out any happiness in your life and kill any hope you have of a spontaneous fun night out.

But this outdated view of a budget changed for me once my husband, Josh, and I finally set one up.

I told you earlier how Josh and I left our big law firm jobs to start our own law firm and pursue our **If Life Were Perfect** vision. Keep in mind this happened smack in the middle of a recession and as our fourth child was born, so the timing was impeccable.

While we were very intentional about creating our vision for the life we ultimately wanted, we were not as intentional when it came to financially planning for it. We learned very quickly that an unfunded dream is merely a wish, and that if we were going to make the dream come true, we had to take charge of our finances that were spiraling out of control.

We had gone from having those big law firm checks to pouring money into a brand-new business with little income initially coming in. Month after month in the infancy stages of our business, we watched as our bank account balances went down, while our credit card balances went up. There were two main reasons for this: (1) our monthly business expenses for our new law firm were exceeding our monthly profits, and (2) we had not downgraded our lifestyle to adjust to our new incomes.

Soon it felt like our finances had taken on a life of their own, and my husband and I began blaming each other. I felt like he was controlling our purchases and deciding what was a legitimate expense (like fantasy football), and he felt like I was not taking personal responsibility for our financial bottom line. (I thought he should figure it out as I had my hands full with the baby and kids.) We were both living with tension and anxiety, and we worried about how we could provide. At one point, I even pleaded with my husband to just go back to working for a law firm, even if it meant he would be unhappy.

Things finally came to a head one afternoon when I stopped by Nordstrom to pick up a gift for a friend. I called Josh about something else, and he was not happy to hear I was out shopping. He brought up our finances once again and I finally asked just how much credit card debt we were in. Obviously, after hearing the number, no purchases were made that day! We were in major financial trouble and I knew we had to do something fast or risk losing everything we had been working so hard for.

After wanting to throw up, I was finally ready to face our finances. It was less about courage in that moment and more about a sheer will to survive. I knew we needed to pay for our family. I knew it was time to stop spending money on things that we did not need. And I knew it was time for us both to stop blaming each other. In other words, I knew it was time to set up a budget!

No more waking up with anxiety every morning thinking of the finances.

No more panicking over every single purchase or feeling guilty for swiping a card.

No more fearing financial failure that could keep us from achieving our dreams.

And no more fighting with each other over money!

I am going to share with you what I did next, because it changed everything for us.

It is a process I did organically, but now teach at my workshops. It is such a simple process and I know it will make a huge difference for you. And it's something that you can do right now from your home. All that is required is a lot of courage and possibly a drink!

THE P.E.A.C.E. PROCESS

Most of the budgets I've come across online are all about numbers and spreadsheets. I see those charts and honestly, I start feeling bored.

But the process I'll be showing you is less about giving things up and more about getting what you want. It's helping you evaluate every dollar you have and seeing how it can help you reach those goals on your **If Life Were Perfect** list.

I teach this budgeting process using the acronym P.E.A.C.E. because that was the end result for us—peace with ourselves because we were honest about what we could afford; peace with each other because we stopped blaming one another and got on the same team; and peace with our finances because we took control and quickly overcame our debt. It worked for us, it works for other families, and I know it will work for you!

P: Print Your Statements

The first thing I did was print out my financial statements. Up until that point, I don't even think I knew the passwords for our accounts, and I certainly was not regularly checking them.

The financial statements I printed out are the ones you probably should, too. They included statements from my banking accounts, brokerage and investments accounts, whole life policies, insurance policies, credit card accounts, retirement accounts, rent/mortgage, student loans, business accounts, and anything else that could provide me clues about where my money was going.

Once I had those statements physically printed out, I finally had a place to begin.

E: Earn, Owe, and Have

I knew there were three key numbers we had to know to understand our finances—what we earned, what we owed, and what we had.

Now, before I explain how to determine these numbers, I'm going to give you a pep talk. Looking at these numbers can be tough for some of us, especially if we're having financial troubles. Seeing these numbers may be as fun as stepping on the scale after the holidays, when even the sweatpants don't fit. But we must know these numbers to know where we are financially, and trust me—together we can and will change them for the better!

What you earn is your monthly income. Your monthly income typically comes from your W-2 if you are an employee, your 1099 if you are an independent contractor, or your average monthly profit after expenses if you are a business owner. It also includes any monthly income you get from the earned interest on your investments, and any other monthly income that you're legally obligated to receive (i.e. child support, government benefits, social security). Add these numbers together, and that is your monthly income.

What you owe is your debt and fixed costs, like your credit card balances, mortgage or rent, student loans, car payments, utility and internet bills, and any other payments you are contractually obligated to make. Add these numbers together, and that is your current total debt.

What you have is the value of your assets and accounts. This typically includes the average balances in your banking and investment accounts or whole life policies, the fair market value of your home and car, your retirement account balances, and any other financial assets. You can use today's fair market value to determine the value of each asset. The fair market value is what you could reasonably sell the asset for as of today. Add these numbers together, and that is what you have.

Now, a final thought for those of you who still can't bear to see these numbers. Research shows that the more we repeat an uncomfortable action, the less anxiety we will feel. So, if seeing these numbers brings you anxiety, then keep looking at them every day!

A: Assign a Grade

Once I had a better understanding of what I earned, owed, and had, I decided to grade my purchases. I took out a pen and assigned a grade of A, B, C, D, or F next to every purchase and expense, with A being awesome and F being Fail. I based the grade on two main factors: a) whether the purchase was a necessity, and b) whether I could get it for less.

I recall that the first F I gave was for cable tv, because it was not a necessity, and we never used it. That eighty dollars I was paying each month was basically like burning money. Marketing programs we bought for work only got a C. While the programs weren't bad, they weren't being implemented, so the monthly fee didn't make sense. Even our local grocery store got a C because, while food was a necessity, I could easily get it for less if I was willing to drive to Costco. You get the idea.

When all was said and done, there were very few As. Seeing the grades next to every single purchase helped me visually see where changes should be made. You'll be surprised at how many dollars slip out of your hands every month on things you don't really need or can easily get for less. Even if you aren't having financial problems, you should go through this grading exercise to maximize your money. Why not pick up those dollars left on the table and use them for something you really want?

C: Chop and Change

One of my favorite shows is the Food Network's *Chopped*. If you haven't seen it, it's a program in which four chefs compete to make dishes out of strange food items, with one chef getting eliminated after each round. When it's time to cut a chef, the judges put that chef's dish on the chopping block and then tell them, "Chef, you've been chopped!" This is usually right after you hear their sob story of why they need the grand prize money.

Well, that's what happened to any purchase or expense on my graded list that did not get an A. It was "chopped" from our monthly budget or changed in some way to save us more money. By chopping or changing our purchases and expenditures, we literally reduced our monthly budget by thousands of dollars!

I even went so far as to chop our son's beloved tutor, Bob. That was when my husband thought I had officially lost my mind. He made me bring back poor Bob from the chopping block. But other than Bob, almost everything else was chopped or changed.

Now, just because you're chopping and changing doesn't mean it's forever. You can always bring back all the fun things when you're in a financial place to afford or enjoy them. Now when I take a trip or buy myself something nice, I don't have to feel guilty or hesitate, because I've budgeted for it, and I can now afford it.

E: Eliminate or Reallocate

Because my husband and I were in so much credit card debt, we agreed that any extra money we brought in each month above our now much smaller monthly expenses would go to pay off our credit cards. (If you don't have credit card bills, that is awesome, you can use the extra money toward other financial goals we'll be talking about soon.) Josh and I also agreed during this process that any new purchases we made would only be with cash. We literally locked up our credit cards as though they didn't exist.

At first, making changes to our spending was hard, but the benefits that came were unreal. I can't explain how empowering it felt to watch our credit card balances shrink. Month after month, by sticking to our much leaner budget, we would throw any extra cash at paying the balances down. The feeling it brought was so incredible that no purchase I had given up could possibly compete. We also saw the conflict in our marriage slowly decrease. Josh and I were finally on the same team and working toward a common goal.

I can't remember the exact day, but I do remember the moment when Josh showed me our final credit card statement and the balance was completely paid off. It was a very happy moment between us, and we felt so much relief and joy. Because we had pulled that off, I knew that together, we could do anything.

As we'll talk about in the upcoming chapters, continuing to stick with a budget can help you pay off your debts and build your wealth. It worked for us, and I know it can work for you. By taking control of our finances, we realized that vision on our **If Life Were Perfect** list and overcame our debt and built our financial security. We never did end up bringing cable back!

I want you to have that feeling where you're finally in control of your money. By following the P.E.A.C.E. process and sticking with it, you can reach any financial goal. Don't let anything, especially your finances, get between you and what you really want!

3

PAYING OFF DEBT

DID YOU KNOW THAT 87 percent of us Gen X and Millennial parents are in debt?[4] That's a lot of us who owe someone money for something! The reason for our debts may vary, but can you guess what the top four offenders are? If you thought credit cards, car loans, student loans, and mortgages, then you are right!

The bigger question is: Do *you* owe money for any of these things? If so, it is time to pay off your debts!

Obviously, if us parents could have afforded to pay cash for the top four offenders and other needs, we probably would have done so in the first place. I am also going to guess that if we could turn back time, there are many things we would not have spent money on when we did not have cash for them that were not necessities.

Avoiding debt in the first place is, well, the best way not to have debt! It kind of reminds me of that abstinence talk we all got in high school about the safest way to never have an unplanned pregnancy. Now, realistically, we all know that most of us are probably going to end up having ... debt. Which means we must figure out the role it will play in our financial journey.

I'll never forget working at the GAP in college when a young woman my age came in and swiped three credit cards to pay for clothes until one of them went through. If you think we have outgrown this type of reckless spending now that we are parents, we have not. Now we do it for bigger things, like leasing a car we cannot afford, or charging a vacation because we don't have the cash.

We also do it for the "good things" in life, like buying a home or trying to start a business, only to find that that debt eventually explodes and becomes a death sentence for our dream.

We have also relied too much on debt to help us get through the storms in life when we needed savings and insurance protections instead.

Regardless of whether you see yourself as a victim of your choices or a victim of your circumstances when it comes to your debt, too many of us are borrowing money to pay for things we simply cannot afford.

Now you're thinking, aren't you the person who just told us readers: make your **If Life Were Perfect** list and use your money to get what you really want?

Yes, I did. But the operative word is *your*. Use *your* money and not money you've borrowed!

We know full well we can never fully enjoy things if we are worried about the cost. Nothing is worth having at the cost of drowning in debt or being dishonest with ourselves over what we can afford.

I had a client whose dream was to drive a sports car. He told me how he got an incredible "deal" on his car, when in fact it involved abnormally long and hefty monthly car payments. When I looked at his finances, he had not hit many of the financial milestones that other families had. His wife shared with me how much anxiety he felt over their finances. I felt bad for him because he'd tried to reach a personal dream with money he did not have, and it was costing him dearly.

Too many of us are trying to hit important life milestones or realize dreams with money we simply do not have. While I want to see all of us realize our **If Life Were Perfect** list, we have to do what it takes to get there and live honestly within our means.

We may need a car for our family, but do we need *that* car?

We may need housing for our family, but do we need *that* house?

We may need a vacation with our family, but do we need *that* vacation?

I promise you that by following the Three Ps that form the structure of this book—Plan, Protect, and Players—you can eventually get *that* car, *that* house, and *that* vacation, and financially weather those unexpected life events like a layoff or an illness. But you cannot skip over the Three Ps to get there.

If you really want to get rid of debt and work toward what you want, you must understand what debt truly is as a force. It does far more than just demanding money owed to it.

Debt assures you that you need it to buy something "essential."

Debt convinces you that you need it to buy something you "deserve" or want.

Debt sneaks its way into your life, often at your most vulnerable moments.

Debt disguises itself through false promises like "low interest rates" or "no money down," making you think it is harmless.

Debt swears to you that without it, you can never function in the modern world.

And finally, once debt works its way into your life, it is nearly impossible to show it the door.

Debt is like a terrible guy you would never want to hang around! Let's look deeper at what it costs us by having a relationship with debt.

UNDERSTANDING INTEREST

One of debt's trickiest ways of invading our lives is to mask itself through the promise of a harmless "low interest rate."

Most of us understand that when we borrow money, it comes with interest, which means we must ultimately pay back the principal plus the interest that accrued.

Interest is either *simple* interest, which is calculated based on a percentage of the loan, or it's *compounding* interest, where it's calculated based on a percentage of the loan, plus the previously accrued interest incorporated back into the principal. It's important to understand how interest is calculated for any of your debts, and how it can dramatically increase the amount you must pay back compared to what you initially borrowed.

For example, let's say you took out a thirty-year fixed mortgage on your home for $500,000 with a 3 percent interest rate. By the time you make your last payment, you will have paid back $758,887 (the original balance, plus *simple* interest.) How can an extra $258,887 from that "low interest rate" possibly be called harmless?

Interest applies to any debt that comes with an interest rate—your mortgage, your student loans, your car payments, and your credit cards. How many of us signed up for a credit card with promises of cash back or frequent flyer miles and a "low interest rate," only to watch that interest rate spike once the promotional period ends or when we've missed a payment? I've seen credit card rates spike from 0 percent to 22 percent without people even realizing it. You can see how people get crushed by debt, and how there's really no such thing as a "low interest rate!"

If you are starting to freak out a little about your debts and how interest works, then I already consider this chapter mission accomplished. We should all be freaking out and avoiding debt if possible!

On the flip side, you'll read in the investment section of this book about how your investments typically accrue interest, meaning that your original investment will substantially grow over time. That's because in that scenario you are the "lender," and not the "borrower" like you are now when you have debt! As my accountant says, interest can be your worst enemy or your best friend, depending on which way it swings!

For this reason, we need to get you from the red (owing money) over to the black (growing your money) as soon as possible! We will tackle your highest interest rate debts first (typically your credit cards), then your car payment, then your student loan payment, and conclude with the typically lowest interest rate offender (your mortgage) to put an end to the financial trap of debt once and for all.

As a fair side note, some financial experts say it is better to take on debt, if you can invest your cash instead for a higher return than what you are losing paying in interest on your debt. It's a calculated game that mathematically may make sense, and I have personally seen it work for families. The problem is that most of us don't understand how to play this game, nor do we have the discipline to make every right play. Plus, when a problem comes along—like a job loss, catastrophe, or death—suddenly you don't have a full deck of cards and you find yourself loosing badly.

Here is the honest truth: most of us parents are not going into debt because of a well thought out calculated strategy, but rather because we are paying for things we simply cannot afford. As you read through this entire book, you'll have a much better understanding of how debts and investments work, so you can make the best choices for your family going forward.

If you remember nothing else from this book, do not forget how interest works!

THE TRUTH ABOUT YOUR CREDIT RATING

Another factor that determines the pain of your debt is your credit rating.

Your credit rating is issued by the three main credit bureaus— Experian, Equifax, and TransUnion—and is primarily determined by how much debt you have accrued through the years and your reliability in paying those debts off. Statistically, most of us parents have a fair to good credit score, with the average credit rating of 680 (but don't high five yourself yet).[5]

The higher the credit rating, the easier it gets to secure new loans with better interest rates and lower finance charges. A high credit rating shows potential lenders that you are reliable, as historically you've paid back your debts on schedule. Obviously, a lower credit rating makes it more difficult to secure new loans, and results in higher interest rates and higher finance charges on new loans. Isn't that ironic? The worse financial position you are in, the more you will have to pay.

Let's go back to the mortgage example again so you can see how your credit score can affect the terms of a loan. I told you how if you took out a thirty-year fixed mortgage on your home for $500,000 with a 3 percent interest rate, by the time you pay it all back, you will actually have to pay back $758,887 (because of the interest).

Now let's say that your credit rating is poor, so the lender will not give you the 3 percent interest rate that they are giving to those of us with good credit. Instead the lender gives you a 3.5 percent interest rate because they view you as less likely to pay them back. With the higher interest rate, you will have to pay back $808,280, as opposed to the $758,887 those with a good credit rating pay. Why? Because you have a higher interest rate. That's almost a $50,000 penalty for having poor credit!

So how do we end up with poor credit? It happens for a number of reasons, including defaulting on a loan, having too much debt, and ironically, for not ever taking on debt (since there is no debt history to evaluate in determining your reliability.)

Having poor credit can affect far more than just your interest rates on your loans. It can prevent you from even qualifying for a loan in the first place. It can also affect your ability to rent a home, and it can reduce your employment opportunities because employers can ask for your written consent to check your credit rating to determine your ability to manage finances. In other words, poor credit can affect your finances and your future!

I shared with you earlier how Josh and I were drowning in credit card debt while we were building our business. Ironically, we have both always had outstanding credit ratings because we never missed payments. I share this with you because I want you to understand something that so many people miss:

Having a good credit rating does not mean you are good at managing your finances. It only means you are good at managing your debts!

Some financial experts really take issue with the fact that our society determines our financial reliability, and even rates us, based on our doing something we should be avoiding in the first place—borrowing someone else's money to pay for something we cannot afford, i.e. debt.

I won't spent too much time debating the legitimacy of how credit ratings are issued, but my goal here is for you to fully understand how your credit rating is affecting the terms of your current debts and any new debts I hope to convince you not to take on in the future (with the possible exception of a fifteen-year fixed-rate mortgage).

If you'd like to check and see what your current credit rating is, you can request it online from any of the big three credit agencies—Experian, Equifax, and TransUnion. You can also sign up to receive ongoing reports. (There is an art to checking your credit rating, since pulling it too often or through the wrong methods can lower your credit rating.) Also, be sure to regularly monitor your credit rating to ensure that you have not inadvertently failed to pay someone, and that no one has stolen your credit.

Now that we understand what debt really is, and how the interest rates and credit ratings are affecting our debts, let's get ready to tell debt it's over, this time for good!

PAYING OFF YOUR CREDIT CARDS

We hear a lot about student loans being a huge financial burden, but did you know that there are more parents who have credit card debt than have student loans?[6] Too many of us are relying on credit cards to pay for things we cannot afford.

I cannot tell you how many times people have confided in me that they are having massive financial problems, only to then see them swiping their credit cards to pay for things they do not need, or things they say they need yet cannot afford.

Credit card debt can ruin far more than just your finances. I have personally seen it ruin families and futures as well. It can also cause us to live in a constant state of anxiety, preventing us from enjoying daily life.

I hope you are not the parent who wakes up in the morning thinking about your growing credit card debt instead of the new day to come.

I hope you are not the parent who feels shame as you swipe your card to pay for that toy when you take your child to the store.

I hope you are not the parent whose heart races and trembles when the credit card statement arrives.

And I really hope you are not the parent who just swipes and clicks and ignores the growing balance because it has gotten *that* out of control.

I understand all those feelings and how easy it is to experience credit card debt firsthand. I am not here to judge you. I am here to help you pay it off.

Most financial experts agree that the first debt you should pay off is your credit card debt. It often comes with the highest interest rates in comparison to other debts and easily increases with every swipe or click. Credit card debt is a huge barrier to reaching the goals on your **If Life Were Perfect** list—those things you really want most!

Are you ready to get rid of those credit card debts once and for all? Are you ready to say yes to having a huge weight lifted off your shoulders? Are you ready to stop that terrible feeling of anxiety once and for all? I'll answer that for you: Yes! You are!

Fight with Every Possible Dollar

If you want a fighting chance at paying off your credit cards, the first thing you will need to do is fight with every dollar. Paying the minimum monthly payment on your credit card balances is not enough, as such payments mostly go toward paying off the newly accrued interest, and not the actual principal.

If you did not come up with a lot of extra money when you set up your new budget, go back again and again until every single dollar is 100 percent going to your bare minimum needs, and whatever is left is going toward paying off your credit cards. I promise you that no coffee or new blouse will bring you as much joy as getting closer to your ideal life. No concert or fine wine will be as wonderful as waking up that first morning after your debt is paid off and having that weight lifted off your shoulders.

Increasing your income will also help you fight debt, and I'll address it in an upcoming chapter. I'll help you think about if you can ask for a raise, change jobs, have a side hustle, rent or sell your car, or use a bonus. While we must focus on cutting every possible expense to fight credit card debt, it's just as important to see if we can increase income.

One thing you should not cut out is contributing to your employer-matched retirement funds, even when you have credit card debt. It's a mistake people often make—and we'll be discussing it more in the retirement chapter. When an employer matches your contribution, even if it is not a full 100 percent, it's still free money and is an immediate return on your investment. Plus, the sooner you get started contributing to your employer matched retirement fund, the more time the interest compounds on that contribution.

If you're having trouble giving something up in your budget that truly isn't a necessity and with the absolute best value, know that the giving-up is not forever. Once your credit card debt is gone, we can bring some of those fun things back! Besides, nothing is really that fun when you are broke.

Lock Up Your Credit Cards

The next step is to lock up your credit cards! Physically remove them from your access and do not use them under any circumstance! Some people even cut them up.

Trying to pay off your credit card debt while continuing to charge new expenses is like trying to patch holes in a boat while simultaneously drilling new ones—it is total insanity, plus you will sink!

Instead of using credit cards going forward, you are now going to use cash. It will require some day to day changes, but you will get used to them fast. The self-respect and euphoric feeling that will come each time you pay down your credit card debts will far outweigh whatever you are temporarily missing.

Paying with cash means that you will need to plan before you go to a store so you know how much cash you will need. I don't want you to swipe a debit card for now, even though it comes out of your cash accounts, because this is about changing habits, and we need to break you of that swipe-and-go pattern!

You will need to bring cash for other outings as well. I had lunch with a lawyer a few years ago and when the bill came, she pulled out an envelope from her purse stuffed with cash. She told me that every purchase she makes comes from that envelope, and that it is meticulously earmarked for different types of purchases. She, like a handful of my clients, are hardcore followers of financial guru Dave Ramsey, who advises people to pay with cash. It actually pained me to watch her part with her cash so much that I wanted to cover her meal! It also made me realize just how expensive sushi is.

The next change you'll need to make involves your online payment options. It's time to connect them to your cash accounts rather than your credit cards. While it is true that your credit cards have more protections for fraud, and it is easier for you to dispute a fraudulent charge than recoup stolen cash, I will assume your cash accounts don't have much in them if you are in credit card debt! Plus, you are more likely to swipe or click out of habit right now than you are to be the victim of online theft. If I were you, I'd take that risk.

You also need to figure out how to avoid buying things online you do not absolutely need. If buying things you cannot afford goes beyond just normal temptation, consider talking with a therapist or a friend to get to the bottom of this urge.

We will talk in a minute about what to do with those credit cards once they are locked up, and why we may not be canceling them, even though we wish we could!

Determine Which Card Gets Paid Off First

The next thing we need to figure out is where all your credit card debt is. Is it on one card, two cards, three cards?

Once we identify how many cards you have, we must figure out which one should get paid off first. This primarily comes down to a game of math, taking into account not just today's balance, but also what that balance will grow to become with the continuing interest by the time you can fully pay it off. Most of us need help with this analysis, and there are online credit card repayment calculators that assist you with determining what the real balance is for each card, considering those factors.

Once you have those numbers, you can identify which card is really costing you the most in comparison to others. That's the card we will want to focus on first!

Now, some people with multiple credit cards consider transferring them all onto one single card with a lower interest rate. The idea is that this can save them money in the end.

Many of us have gotten caught up in this balance transfer game when we found ourselves falling more and more into credit card debt. We played "hot potato," continually transferring the balances on our credit cards onto new cards to get a lower interest rate. This is problematic. Opening new cards can negatively affect your credit rating, and usually that "low interest rate" promotional period on the new card will end. Eventually, you'll get stuck and find that someone wants to get paid!

When you evaluate whether it makes sense (or if it's possible) to transfer all your credit card balances onto a single card with a lower rate with the purpose of now paying it all off, you must do the proper math and make sure it makes financial sense. You would also never want to transfer a card that has a lower interest rate onto a card with a now larger balance and larger interest rate!

You also need to understand how your interest rate can change if you miss a payment or the promotional interest rate term expires, especially if now you have one large balance on that card. You also must find out if there are transfer fees for rolling all your balances onto one card. You need to understand how late fees will be applied if you are late on a payment. This all must get factored in your final decision on whether to consolidate your credit card debts.

Beyond interest rates, there's an emotional component that must be factored into your analysis as well. I shared with you how paying off our credit cards gave Josh and I an addictive sense of accomplishment and freedom. Paying off one card was a huge boost to our self-esteem and confidence, proving to ourselves that we could tackle the next one. We also had these euphoric feelings when each card was paid off, the kind of happiness that a random-purchase happiness could never compete with.

For these reasons, when you consider the order of paying off your cards, or consolidating to one card, you should not only consider the interest rates and overall cost when prioritizing, but also whether the order of payoff will bring you those great feelings along the way. If you start with the card that has the highest balance, will you burn out halfway through? Or is it more likely that if you start with the lower balance card and pay that off first, those grand emotions will motivate you to tackle the bigger credit card next? Understand the role your emotions will play in this credit card elimination journey.

Finally, do not, and I repeat, do not, under any circumstance take equity out of your home to pay off your credit card debts! If you default on your credit cards, they can close your account and go through a whole messy process to try to make you pay, but if you roll these credit card debts into your mortgage, and then default on your mortgage payments, they can take your home!

Get Ready to Battle

Now that you know what credit card to tackle first (or you have just a single card that you need to address), it is time to battle hard.

I know that if it were only as simple as setting up a budget and then using extra money to pay off each of your credit cards one by one until each one was gone, then everyone would do it. The truth is, your emotions and habits are far more likely than your actual financial means to sabotage your desire to be credit card-free. I would compare paying off debt to dieting and exercising. You have your caloric-intake and exercise plan, you have your goal, you have the ability now that you stocked up on healthy foods and purchased your fitness gear, but will you have the willpower to see it through?

You know yourself best, so come up with a plan that you think will keep the wind in your sails. Also consider creating arbitrary milestones, like paying off half the card, for example, if the balance is large, so you can feel that sense of accomplishment that will motivate you to pay off the rest.

Your emotions and discipline in paying off your debt will be the driving force in all of this. Go back to your **If Life Were Perfect** list, remember what you really want most, set up the budget, and then please pay off those credit cards immediately!

Once You Are Credit Card Free

If you just follow everything we have talked about up until this point, you absolutely can become credit card free. While the length of time it will take depends on the amount you owe, the extra money you've found in your budget, and your new efforts to increase your income, it can and will happen if you stick to the process.

Can you imagine how good that moment is going to feel once you finally do it?

The moment you pay off your credit cards is a huge milestone you should never forget. And that's because it should become a milestone that you should never experience again!

In an ideal world, you would lock up your credit cards forever, close out your accounts, and never use them again. But in the real world and because of the way credit plays into so many aspects of society and everyday life, it is probably not practical to never need them again.

Unfortunately, closing out your credit cards will likely negatively affect your credit rating. Why? Because the big three credit bureaus rate you higher when you continually use credit and then pay it off in a timely manner.[7]

Closing out your credit cards could affect your ability to book a car rental or a hotel room, or other similar types of incidentals, although many institutions have gotten better about allowing you to secure your reservation with cash or a debit card.

Closing out your credit cards can also expose you to fraud, as I mentioned earlier, since there are many protections our government affords credit card holders that may not extend to, say, your personal debit card. For this reason, my accountant insists that many of my automatic payments are tied to a credit card rather than my cash accounts.[8]

Credit cards, no matter how much you want to leave them behind forever, will likely play a role throughout your financial journey because the rest of society values them.

Credit cards are salty and sweet. But you should never, under any circumstance, ever use them again to pay for something you cannot immediately pay off.

Now I understand that things happen, people get sick, people lose jobs, and people want things. And in this book, we will cover financially preparing for all those scenarios. At no point should relying on a credit card be the solution.

After your debt is all paid off, if you do choose to go back to having your automatic payments tied to your credit cards for security protections, make sure that your budget already accounts for those purchases. In other words, make sure you have the cash already on hand to immediately pay off your card. This is where many of us stumble, meaning we have the cash set aside, and then we charge the payment on our card, and then some unforeseen thing happens like a job loss or an unexpected expense, and oops, we no longer have the cash to pay off the credit card balance right away.

For these reasons, in this book, I'm going to emphasize the importance of emergency funds savings and other methods for having disposable cash on hand or proper insurance when something unexpected happens.

I've put before you a big task—paying off your credit cards. But I have confidence that you can do it.

One of my all-time favorite movie scenes is from *A League of Their Own*—a classic film about a professional women's baseball league during World War II. The scene features star player Dotty Hinson (Gina Davis) and the team manager Jimmy Duggan (Tom Hanks). Dotty says she's quitting the team, quitting professional baseball, because "it just got too hard."

For many of us parents, with our finances, our families, and all the unexpected storms we have to weather along the way, there will be times when we want to throw up our hands and say "it just got too hard." In those moments when we see a monumental task before us—like paying off those credit cards that have consumed us with anxiety, bitterness, or loss of self-respect—and we want to give up before completion, remember Jimmy Duggan's response in the film.

Duggan turns around looks Dotty Hinson straight in the eye and tells her, "It's supposed to be hard. If it wasn't hard, everyone would do it. The hard is what makes it great."

Paying off your credit cards is going to be hard. And that's why not everybody does it. But it is going to feel GREAT when you've accomplished it. In fact, it's going to feel GREAT every time you see those credit card balances diminish.

THE FAMILY NEST EGG

You are not going to be the statistic anymore! You are now the other guy, a new person when it comes to credit cards—no longer relying on them and no longer controlled by them.

Go back again and again to your **If Life Were Perfect** list. Remember how freedom from credit cards will get you closer to what you want most in life and know that all us parents are cheering you on.

And I promise you again, that moment when the last card is paid off, it really will be GREAT!

PAYING OFF YOUR CARS

We talked earlier about the top four household debt offenders—credit cards, car loans, student loans, and mortgages. Your car loan is the next logical debt to tackle after your credit cards are paid off because it typically has a higher interest rate compared to your student loans and mortgage.

While tackling this debt is critical, it should not be done exclusively or instead of investing, paying for life milestones, or building your emergency reserve, which we'll explore in the chapters ahead. Don't worry right now about the best order for achieving these milestones. In the Players section of the book, I will help you understand who can help you put together a personalized timeline that makes sense for you.

I also want to encourage you still to live within your leaner budget so you have extra money to pay off your car while working toward other financial goals. Once the credit card debt is gone, it may feel tempting to relax your budget or feel complacent about other debts. We need to keep that winning attitude and those euphoric feelings going until all your debts are gone! The good news is that it gets easier and easier to pay off debt, because you'll have more money freed up after erasing previous debt.

Now, it's time for us parents to have an honest conversation about how we are financing our cars. While a car itself is a necessity, too many of us are financing cars that we simply cannot afford.[9]

Whether buying or leasing a car, most of us parents seem to have a never-ending car payment: one financing term ends, only for a new one to begin. And some of us are having a hard time keeping up with these never-ending payments. Before COVID-19 hit, reports were showing that a record number of us were ninety days behind on our car payments![10]

We're also changing out our cars too quickly. While the average life span of an automobile is eleven and a half years, most of us only drive ours for six.[11] There's a corollary here: The average car loan is for six years. It suggests that once we finally pay off our auto loan, we already want new wheels! And for those of us who lease instead, we are only driving our car for three or four years tops before replacing it for a new one, and facing yet again another payment cycle.[12]

So why are we continually financing cars we can't really afford, only to swap them out when they have so much life left in them? Why are we wasting so much money that we really need to use for other things? It's time to bust through the lies we are listening to about our car ownership and say enough is enough.

Five Lies from Car Guys
LIE #1: THIS CAR IS AN INVESTMENT

No. If a car salesman tells you this, they're blowing smoke in your face.

There is a reason I chose to put buying a car in the debt pay-off chapter rather than in the section about financing life milestones.

Buying a depreciating asset with no lasting value is never a life milestone. It is a detrimental mistake and it is keeping you from financial security.

Cars are a depreciating asset no matter how you run the math. Most new cars lose 20 to 30 percent of their value just after the first year! By year five, that same car will have lost 60 percent of its initial value.[13] How can you call it an "investment" when you're pouring money into something that loses substantial value over time?

And again, this isn't a one-time financial splurge. It's is a continual cycle for most of us. We keep borrowing money for something that always loses its value.

LIE #2: LEASING IS A BETTER DEAL

Wrong.

It's easy to get sucked into lease deals on the newest fully loaded cars with "attractive" low monthly payments when we can't afford to pay cash to own them. Who wouldn't want to lease a Mercedes when the lease payment only costs a fraction of the monthly cost of buying one?

But when you hear the word lease, I want you to think of the word "waste" instead.

A lease is not ownership, it's borrowing. The cost for the lease itself includes the money down, the dealer fees, the depreciation costs, the interest built into the lease, taxes, and more fees! There is a reason all those fees get buried in the small fine print.

Plus, if you don't carefully stick to the terms of the lease, like driving only the allotted number of miles, you can get stuck with more costs at the end, or worse, having them rolled over into your next lease.

And what do you have to show for your lease when the term expires? Absolutely nothing. You turn in the car or buy it and begin the car financing cycle yet again.

LIE #3: THIS CAR DEAL IS A ONE-TIME OFFER

The ultimate marketing play is to provide a one-time offer followed by a limited time to respond. This offer convinces us that we must act fast, and that we are getting a good deal because we will be paying less than others.

One of my favorite Christmas commercials I see every year is the *December to Remember* ad from a luxury car manufacturer that shows a very happy wife going out to her driveway on Christmas morning to find a brand-new shiny luxury vehicle with a big red bow on top of it. I always think, do husbands really *do* that? The ad is the perfect combo of playing on our emotions (wanting the wife to be happy on Christmas) and luring us in with a one-time limited offer that ends soon. *Don't think*, they're telling us, *just respond right away.*

The car business is notorious for these emotional ads coupled with the one-time limited offers. And these ads come around not only for Christmas, but all the other holidays, and sometimes just because it's a Tuesday! The "one-time limited offer" just rises from the dead again and again!

The truth is that there's always a deal to be made in the car business, and hopefully we can see the irony of taking on debt to take advantage of a "good deal."

LIE #4: THIS CAR HAS A LOW MONTHLY PAYMENT

Remember how we talked about that sneaky little interest rate? Well, that interest gets built into every car financing arrangement, whether through a lease or a purchase!

LOW MONTLY PAYMENT!!! gets splashed across the vehicle or the ad while the overall car cost is buried in the fine print. That's because if we knew what the true monthly cost was for the life of our loan, we would run the other way.

I read an article many years ago that cited one major difference between the middle class and the wealthy as being the middle-class' tendency to focus on the monthly payment for things and the wealthy folk's tendency to only consider the overall cost.

Do not let a low monthly payment deceive you. Rather, focus on the overall cost! Look behind that attractive low monthly payment that masks the high cost of the car—the amount you have to put down, the interest rate, car depreciation, the length of the loan, taxes, and the terms of the loan. That is the only way to understand the true cost and what you will get in the end.

LIE #5: YOU NEED TO DRIVE A NICE CAR

How many times have we married financial success to the idea of owning nice things? How many times have we gauged someone's finances based on the car they drive? How many times have we felt pressure to drive a nice car because we think it's important for our professional or social status?

The truth is that many wealthy people don't drive nice cars. They don't feel the need to impress other people, and they don't see the value in a depreciating asset.

Warren Buffet, whose net worth at the time of this writing is upwards of $80 billion, is notorious for driving his used Cadillac, which was not top-of-the-line.

Sam Walton, who founded Walmart, drove a used Ford pickup truck during his life.

Mark Zuckerberg, whose net worth has reached $100 billion, drives a $30,000 Acura.

Could it be possible that if billionaires don't need nice new cars, that maybe we don't need them either?

Look, most of us don't need to drive expensive cars. When the need *really* arises, or maybe when we want one for a special night out, renting a nice new car for a day or two as opposed to owning or leasing one for your entire adult life can save you a bunch of money in the end.

The Only Way to Buy a "New" Car

Now that we understand the truth and traps around car financing, it is time to rethink how we purchase vehicles going forward. Now

I know this is easier said than done, especially if you live in places where the car culture is real! I have to park my used SUV at my office among Teslas, Maseratis, and even a Lamborghini, so I understand the pressure to fit in! But if we are going to do right by our family and use our hard-earned dollars to secure our future, then we need to eliminate the car trap once and for all.

As you evaluate whether to pay off your current car or sell it and get something less expensive, I want you to first P.A.U.S.E. so you can make the absolute best choices for yourself, your family, and your finances.

P—PAY CASH

Can you pay cash for the car? Too many of us are getting sucked into financing vehicles we really cannot afford. Money is money at the end of the day no matter how much you break it down into small monthly payments.

Some will argue that if you get a low interest rate, you can invest the cash you would have used in a one-time lump-sum purchase and make a higher return. But here's my question for you: Do you have the cash on hand—cash you could easily part with—to pay for a car without derailing other financial goals?

Another question: Can you *really* get a low interest rate and are you *certain* you can invest that money and get a higher return?

Yet another question: Are you positive you won't lose money on your investment?

We need to be honest about the real reason we are financing our cars! I guarantee you will make a much wiser car purchase if you are parting with cash to pay for it.

Now, if paying cash really is impossible, have you considered alternate means of transportation until you can save up for the cheapest, safest car you can pay cash for? If you truly must finance a vehicle, your loan should be for the absolute minimum amount for the shortest period of time possible!

A—AFFORDABLE
Is the car affordable?

Many parents wind up spending $40,000-plus for top-of-the-line cars when they could be saving tens of thousands of dollars by buying a car that is just as dependable for much less. Furthermore, high-end luxury vehicles are more expensive to repair once the warranty expires compared to less expensive brands.

It's vitally important to understand the total cost of ownership over time, including purchase cost, tax, title, repair costs, maintenance, registration, gas or electric charging costs, and hopefully not financing costs! By buying a car that is more affordable, you will save loads of money in the short term and long term.

U—USED
Is the car used?

As I mentioned earlier, new cars drastically depreciate in the first few years of their life. Buying used can save you 60 percent of the cost! Imagine what you could be doing with that money? With the average lifespan of a car being eleven and a half years, imagine the money you can save by buying used at a discounted rate and then driving the car for its remaining lifespan.

Before you buy any vehicle, go online and find out its depreciation rate so you can see in real numbers how much you will save by buying used.

S—SAFE AND RELIABLE
Is the car safe and reliable?

Driving an unsafe car is never worth the risk. We also need a reliable car so we can meet our obligations to others and make it to and from work on time.

Thankfully, with modern technology, many used cars are completely safe and reliable, and you can research their ratings and safety records online. For this reason, it's also important to make sure you are regularly maintaining your vehicle.

E—EXIGENCY (EXTREME NEED OR DEMAND)

This is by far one of the biggest factors when it comes to replacing your car. The #1 reason we get caught up in the never-ending car trap financing cycle is because we buy cars we do not absolutely need with money we don't have!

While yes, we may need a car, do we absolutely need to replace the one we have? Or could we repair or maintain the one we have, and drive it for as long as it is safe and reliable?

Buying a car based on need and NOT want is the exit door for the car financing cycle trap!

Moving Forward with a Car Purchase

If you can honestly answer yes to all the P.A.U.S.E. questions, you can feel confident that paying off the car you are driving or buying a different one with cash really is a well thought out decision.

I know that driving a used car may not feel ideal, but it doesn't have to be forever. Once you are completely on track to meet all of your financial goals, you can always buy something better. And when you are financially set and can afford that dream car on your **If Life Were Perfect** list, you will love it even more knowing you can afford it.

PAYING OFF YOUR STUDENT LOANS

I know there are many feelings and frustrations surrounding student loan debt. In an ideal world we would have never had to borrow money to invest in our education. But here we all are now, as parents, still making payments on those student loans along with all our other bills.

Student loans affect us all differently depending on how we view them. There are the people who keep student loan debt for decades because the interest rates are so low. There are the people who don't want to pay their student loan debt off because they are waiting for the government to step in. There are the people content living with student loan debt because it has become socially acceptable and common. And there are people who make the minimum monthly payment on their student loans while keeping the entire payoff out of sight, out of mind.

No matter how you view your student loan debts, a debt is still a debt! And eventually your debts must get paid!

Did you know that one in four Americans have student loan debt? The average student loan balance owed by an individual is a whopping $37,172.[14] That's the *average*, meaning many of us owe even more than that! Student loan debt follows us into our twenties, thirties, and even forties, with the average payback period being 19.7 years![15] That's twenty years of payments that cannot go toward other things.

I've met too many parents who have stayed at companies or worked for people they detest simply because they need the money to repay their massive student loans. I've met too many couples who had to delay marriage and children because of their student loan debt. I've met too many families who cannot afford to buy a home because of their student loan debt.

But here's what's really scary: 41 percent of us with student loans do not have the money to cover an unexpected bill of $400. That's how crushing student loan debt can be.[16]

Should You Pay Off Your Student Loan Debt Early?

While student loan debt is keeping families from reaching many important financial and life milestones, most of us just chip away at the monthly payment without a strong conviction to pay them off early.

I know a husband who had more than $100,000 in student loans. He was a hard worker, but the nature of his industry was a lot of hustle and gigs, and not a set salary. He and his wife financially struggled at times, sometimes finding it difficult just to afford a roof over their heads. The wife said she began listening to finance podcasts and was inspired to take control of their predicament, including the student loan debt. They lived modestly with their young children, and each time her husband would get an extra project they would make a large payment on the student loan debt. It took a few years for them, but eventually their hard work and dedication paid off and they became student loan-free. Can you imagine how proud they felt? What a huge milestone in their financial journey. The financial discipline skills they developed carried over to reaching other huge milestones as well, like buying a home.

Most of us think of student loan debt as having such low interest rates that they are relatively harmless, but we don't realize how much that adds up during the life of the student loan. That leaves many of us not just throwing money at monthly payments, but interest that can cost us tens of thousands of dollars.

The first step you must take when evaluating whether to pay off your student loans early is to find out what the payoff really is. Not just the monthly payments, but all that interest that has accrued, even during any deferment years. Not every student loan has low interest rates, especially those that were issued by private institutions when we were going through school. Some families are paying 6 percent interest or higher on a student loan balance!

Once you have that number right in front of you, and you can see how much money you will ultimately be paying off given interest, I predict paying off your student loans may feel a little more urgent.

Paying Off Student Loans vs. Other Things

One of the great debates is whether to pay off your student loans early or use that money for other things, like buying a home, starting a business, or saving for retirement.

My husband and I struggled with these decisions. Our combined student loan debt from our respective private law schools was over $100,000. We were torn over whether we should invest more in our growing business, start paying down our new mortgage, or take care of the student loan debt. Or, just say forget it, go to Vegas, and bet it all on black (kidding).

Paying off your student loans early versus investing in other things are choices you too must carefully evaluate.

My husband and I agreed that one of our student loans had to go immediately. It was a private loan with a high interest rate compared to our other ones. We paid this off by continuing to stick to our leaner budget and using our extra money to throw at that debt.

So, now, let's talk about that strict use of the extra money for a moment. When you are going through all this yourself, tackling debt upon debt and investing for your future, it can feel at times like a no-fun, never-ending diet. So, I will be totally honest. Every time we hit a new financial milestone, we would do something special to celebrate. We even took a special trip, knowing that was money that could have gone to other things. You will need to find that sweet spot between enjoying life now and doing your future self a favor by paying off your debts.

Once our private student loan was paid off, we still had a significant amount of student loans issued from the federal government. While the interest rates, yes, were low, they were still quite costly.

This time, my husband and I were not in total sync. He did not think the priority should be to pay off our federal student loans but rather to use the money to invest in our business, the idea being that we could make more of a profit than the cost of the interest on the student loans. Many of our well-educated and financially savvy friends feel the same way.

But for me, the decision to pay off our student loans had a powerful emotional motivation. It bothered me knowing we still owed money on something from years ago; if anything unexpected should happen (and it did with the COVID-19 pandemic), I wanted to know there would be one less payment I'd have to make to survive. I could not fully enjoy traveling and buying things knowing that I had these outstanding student loans, and I could not round out my thirties knowing I would be taking our student loan debt into another decade!

I wanted to know that if, God forbid, we unexpectedly lost everything we had worked so hard for, we could start over together from zero, and not from the pit of debt. (By the way, if you declare bankruptcy in a worst-case scenario, your student loans are almost never forgiven.)

I also felt our student loans were preventing us from properly saving for our own children's college educations. While we had some money set aside and growing for them, we needed to start getting more aggressive. The hybrid approach of paying off our own student loans while saving for theirs may have made sense from a financial standpoint, but it was mentally hard for me to focus on both and feel like we were making a significant impact.

I share this with you because I know you, too, may feel like you're at a crossroads when it comes to your student loans. And if you are married, you and your spouse may not necessarily agree. It will take honest conversations, an open heart, a balance of emotion and logic, and possibly professional guidance to help you make the best choice for your family.

Josh and I decided to meet each other halfway and allocated a set amount to paying off our student loans while continuing to invest in our growing business. Fortunately for us, the investments in our business brought in great returns, which provided more cash to throw at the loans.

For all the debates that we had, one thing we both agreed on in the end was that it was wonderful being student loan-free.

Refinancing Your Loans

One possible shortcut to paying off your student loans is to find out if you can refinance them for a lower interest rate. Make sure, though, that the loan period for repayment is less than the ones on your current loans. Otherwise, you are essentially restarting the clock as though you had taken them out today!

While government-subsidized student loans historically came with low percentage rates, private banks are also now offering competitive financing terms. A favorable debt to income ratio, along with a good credit rating, will be major factors. By refinancing with a lower interest rate and shortening the term of repayment, you'll be saving on all that interest that adds up in the long term. But be aware of a common misstep: not factoring in lender fees. Remember that your math must include the overall total cost to refinance in comparison to the total overall cost of your current student loans (including the interest for the remainder of the loan). Once you know these numbers, you can determine if refinancing makes sense.

There is one more major consideration I want to put on your radar. There has been a lot of talk from Washington about student loan forgiveness. By refinancing through a private loan, you may be forfeiting any future loan forgiveness or federal protections. While I am not a fan of waiting on Washington for change, this possibility should be considered.

Once You Are Student Loan Free

When you make your last student loan payment, that moment is going to be wonderful.

There was one family I remember who had been paying chunks of money on their student loan debt and were almost student loan free. For years they said their dream was to celebrate by eating at an old restaurant in the wife's hometown where many of their favorite memories were made. She said that when I saw a post on Instagram that they'd made it to the Crab Cooker, then I'd know it had finally happened—they'd be student loan free.

I also know of another mom who donated to her college after she paid off her final student loan. She wanted to help the next generation reduce their need for a student loan.

How will you celebrate the moment when you are finally student loan free? How will it feel not to have that student loan hanging out there so you can spend that money on more important things?

Keep that vision of that wonderful moment in your mind as you take this student-loan pay-off step. By sticking with your leaner budget and eliminating your student loan debt you will be one step closer now to fulfilling your **If Life Were Perfect** list.

THE FAMILY NEST EGG

PAYING OFF YOUR MORTGAGE

The final debt many of us must eliminate on our **If Life Were Perfect** journey will be our mortgage. If you have not yet bought a home, I'll be talking a lot in an upcoming chapter on how to buy a home. You'll still want to read this chapter since you will eventually end up here.

Now, let's start with the good news for those of us with mortgages.

First, congrats on hitting a huge life milestone and becoming a homeowner *in progress*! I add the words *in progress* because until we own the home outright, free and clear, we are technically not yet homeowners!

Second, chances are that you will achieve many of the goals on your **If Life Were Perfect** list before your mortgage gets paid off. So don't feel like you must wait several years before your mortgage is paid off to experience some of those other **If Life Were Perfect** goals.

Next, your mortgage is paying for an asset that provides you shelter, one of our most basic needs. While the monetary value of this asset may (or may not) increase in value over time, it provides you a place to raise your family, and unlike renting, you can ultimately sell it for money or pass it on.

Finally, there's a good chance that you opted for a fixed-rate mortgage on your property, meaning that your interest rate won't change when the economy changes. This makes a lot of sense at the time of this writing, when interest rates are historically low. Ninety-five percent of homeowners right now have a fixed-rate mortgage.

But for all this good news about our mortgages, the bad news is that a mortgage is still a debt, even if it is for something as wonderful as a family home. And as you know, debt comes with interest, and debts must get paid!

So, are you ready to get serious about paying off your mortgage?

Why We Need That Winning Attitude

I want to take you back to a previous part of the book where we discussed having a winning attitude when it comes to getting what we really want most—those things on our **If Life Were Perfect** list.

As you pay off all your debts and find you have finally come to tackling your last one—your mortgage—this is probably the easiest one to feel complacency over. It's the easiest debt to let hang out there for the rest of its term and feel perfectly fine chipping away at it each month until it's finally paid off in fifteen, twenty, or even thirty years depending on when you secured your mortgage and what term length you opted for.

But if you're going to be in it to win it when it comes to controlling your finances, and I mean really locking up and securing your family nest egg and having all your money and assets working toward getting you those things on your **If Life Were Perfect** list, then you are going to have to get serious about paying off your mortgage, even if other families are not.

One of our most basic needs as human beings is to have a roof over our head. I often hear from clients who own their home outright and no longer have a mortgage how secure they feel knowing that they will always have a place for them and their loved ones that is completely theirs. I also hear from clients who are planning for the worst-case scenarios in life, who want to make sure they have enough life insurance in place so that if they prematurely pass away, their mortgage can be paid off. They want that peace of mind of knowing that if they are no longer on this earth, their spouse and kids have a home that is 100 percent theirs.

And I hear from families about how amazing it is, once their final mortgage payment is made, to use that monthly mortgage money on other things. They can save it, invest it, spend it, or whatever else they want. The monthly mortgage payment is typically the largest of a family's expenses. What would you do with that extra money each month if it weren't going toward your mortgage?

But until you make that final mortgage payment, that home is not completely yours and you aren't freed up to use your money on other things. And if you default on your mortgage for whatever reason, the bank can typically take it away and sell it, leaving you displaced and in danger of not having one of your most basic needs as a human being.

I don't know what the future really holds for you, or for anyone else. But wouldn't it be great to know that no matter what, you will have a roof over your head? Don't be complacent about letting this debt hang out there or about chipping away at it over time. Get that winning attitude toward paying off that mortgage.

What's Keeping Us from Paying Off Our Mortgages Sooner?

While owning a home outright free and clear, and no longer having a mortgage, is an ideal scenario for many families, most of us are making huge mistakes with our finances that keep us from paying off our home.

MISTAKE #1: WE BELIEVE OUR "EXTRA MONEY" IS BETTER SPENT PAYING OFF OTHER THINGS

The biggest reason I hear families cite for not aggressively paying off their mortgage beyond the monthly minimum payment is that they believe that extra money would be better spent on other things, like paying off other debts or investing.

Most financial experts agree that paying off other debts, especially ones with higher interest rates, makes more financial sense than spending extra money paying down your mortgage. I completely agree that your mortgage is typically the last debt you should pay off in comparison to other debts with higher interest rates.

I've also seen too many families make the fatal mistake of rolling their other debts into their mortgage, which means that debt now becomes secured by their home. If the new higher or longer mortgage payment becomes unmanageable and they default on their mortgage payments, their lender can foreclose on their home. If they had not rolled those debts into their mortgage and thereby secured it with their home, then it's unlikely the creditor can force a property sale to collect.

As for whether you should invest versus paying off your mortgage sooner, the honest answer is that it really depends. You should compare the probable return on an investment over time to what you will save in interest by paying your mortgage off early. One thing to keep in mind, though, is that investments can go up or down over time. Paying off your mortgage, however, means you are basically guaranteed to own a real asset (your home) that meets a basic human need—shelter. What's more important to you?

We will talk in the Players section about how you can build your personal financial team to help you run those numbers and prioritize so you can make the best decision when it comes to paying off your mortgage earlier versus using that extra money to invest instead. Many people do choose to do a combination of both, where they make extra mortgage payments while also investing.

MISTAKE #2: WE ARE USING OUR HOME EQUITY AS OUR PERSONAL ATM

The next reason families don't pay off their mortgage sooner is because they use the equity in their home to pay for other things.

The equity in your home is simply the difference between what you owe on your home, and what the home could reasonably be sold for (its fair market value). As people begin to pay down the mortgage, or as home values go up, or a combination of both, people begin to accrue equity in their home. But rather than high five themselves when this occurs and feel good about the growing equity in their home, they refinance their home, or take out a loan against their home, and use that equity on other things. This is the equivalent of a football team gaining yards toward the end zone only to be sent back to where they began.

There are different reasons that people pull the equity out of their home. I have seen people justify this for what they claim are "good reasons," like paying off credit cards, paying for their kids' colleges, paying off their cars, paying off their student loans, starting a business, or investing in other things. And for every bad story you may also hear a good one. So how do you know what is best?

In all these scenarios, regardless of good intentions, people are using the equity in their home like a personal ATM to fund other things they do not otherwise have the money for. They are essentially gambling with the roof over their head, rather than with other money that is not literally tied to their home. Why would we take such a risk?

I knew a mother who began refinancing her family's home on a somewhat regular basis back in the mid 2000s when home prices were drastically rising in value. She had very "good reasons" to do this. One time she used the equity she pulled out to pay for remodeling of the home, rather than saving up for the work. Another time she pulled out equity to pay off her credit cards, rather than setting up a budget and using the extra cash to pay those off. Another occasion she got hit with a job loss, and rather than having saved up money for an emergency reserve, she relied on the equity in her home.

Can you guess what the problem was with her approach? Eventually there was no more equity in her home. It kind of reminds me of that beloved children's book *The Giving Tree*, when all that's left of the tree is a stump!

Eventually, when the 2009 financial crisis hit and home values drastically declined, this mother could no longer afford her high monthly mortgage payment and owed more than the home was worth. She defaulted on her payments and the bank foreclosed on her home. This was a horrible ordeal for the entire family. Not only were they broke, they had also lost their place to live.

I won't dispute that there are families who have pulled equity out of their home and had it turn out just fine. But at the end of the day, borrowing money, even if it is against your home, to pay for things you can't otherwise afford, is probably not a risk you should be willing to take.

MISTAKE #3: WE KEEP HITTING THE "RESET" BUTTON

Another reason we fail to pay off our mortgage sooner is because we are constantly hitting the "reset" button on the length of the loan. As people continually refinance to take advantage of lower interest rates or to pull out equity to pay for other things, they often refinance for a new loan that is for the same length of time as their original loan.

For example, if you bought your home in 2015 with a thirty-year repayment term, and then in 2020 refinanced for another thirty-year repayment term, then you've essentially added five years to the amount of time to pay off your home. Plus, that extra five years also means an extra five years of interest.

For this reason, if you do go to refinance, which I will make the case for in a minute, you must secure a new loan that does not reset the clock! This means that if you bought a home five years ago with a thirty-year repayment term, and now choose to refinance, your new loan should not be for a thirty-year repayment term, but for a twenty-five-year term or less. We will talk in a moment about the benefits of securing a shorter-term mortgage versus making extra payments on your current mortgage.

How to Pay off Your Mortgage Quicker

Once we get serious about paying down our mortgage and stop making the mistakes we just talked about, like thinking it's fine to wait to pay down our mortgage, or constantly restarting the clock, or pulling out the equity to pay for other things, it's go time!

I have three very important questions. The answers—if given truthfully—will get you closer to paying down your mortgage, saving a boat load of interest, and truly owning your home.

FIRST QUESTION: WHAT IS THE REAL PAYOFF AMOUNT FOR YOUR MORTGAGE?

Most people can tell you the monthly payment amount for their mortgage, what they bought the home for, how much money they put down as a down payment, and what the interest rate was to the best of their memory. But very few of them could tell you how much money they will have paid back at the end of their loan versus what they initially borrowed.

This is critical because once you see that real number, you are not going to like it. That's because the number encompasses not just the amount you borrowed, but all the interest from that "low interest rate" over the life of the loan, and all the other fees that may get buried into the loan—like closing costs, realtor fees, points, taxes, title, etc.

Going back to an example I gave you earlier in this book, if you took out a thirty-year fixed rate mortgage on your home for $500,000 with a 3 percent interest rate, by the time you pay it all back, you will actually be paying back $758,887.

That's an extra $258,887 because of the interest, on top of the initial loan! Plus all those other fees!

I hope you are thinking what I am thinking—*What is the total dollar amount I really owe on my loan, and how can I get it lower?*

SECOND QUESTION: CAN YOU AFFORD YOUR HOME?

Once you know the real cost of ownership for your home under your current loan, it is time to get honest about whether you can really afford your home.

While many of us may need to finance our home, too many families are what we call house poor. That means we have more than the recommended 28 percent of our gross (pre-tax) monthly income going toward our monthly house payment and more than 36 percent of our gross monthly income going toward our total monthly debts (i.e. monthly mortgage payment, credit card payments, monthly student loan payments, and monthly car payments combined).[17] This should serve as a preliminary warning: if you are outside these 28 percent and 36 percent parameters, you need to further evaluate.

If you find that you are overwhelmed by your mortgage or can't meet other financial obligations or goals, one drastic and obvious way to eliminate your mortgage is to sell your home. I know it is not the ideal, but for some of the families I have worked with, it was the right move (literally!).

I knew one family who had a daughter headed off to college. The parents had put the oldest two children through already and realized that if they sold their current home and were willing to buy another home in a less expensive neighborhood, they could cover their college-bound daughter's tuition. In their mind, they were still getting a great comparable home while also meeting their financial goal of paying for their daughter's higher education. This decision brought them a lot of happiness and peace of mind.

I also worked with a family who had a beautiful estate in the hills, only to realize when they hit their mid-fifties that they had not adequately saved for retirement and had been spending far more than they were making. Initially, this couple strongly opposed the idea of selling their family home and downsizing for something less expensive. For them, this recommendation by their financial planner felt like a personal failure and social suicide. Ultimately, they followed her advice and downsized, and they felt so much better living within their means. Their young adult children were not embarrassed—as the parents feared—but were proud of them for taking control of their finances.

When you consider these stories, along with the 28/36 mortgage rule, and other personal factors, can you really afford your home? If not, would you consider talking with a financial professional about whether it is best to sell, as these families did? Be sure to factor in any tax consequences as well.

THIRD QUESTION: CAN YOU REFINANCE FOR A QUICKER PAYOFF?

One major way to pay off your mortgage sooner is to refinance your current mortgage. Refinancing means you secure a new mortgage with more favorable terms than your original mortgage so you will pay less in interest by either getting a lower interest rate, shortening the length for repayment, or a combination of both. Refinancing can make a huge difference from taking you from being a homeowner *in progress* to a real homeowner.

Here's what to consider for a refinance:

What is the total cost for a refinance?

When you look into refinancing, do not be surprised if lenders or online mortgage calculators are only showing you the interest rate, length of the loan, and monthly mortgage payment. Eventually they will have to show you the additional costs on a line item sheet. These are closing costs, points, taxes, and so on, but those things typically get buried in the conversation as much as possible.

Here is what you need to focus on: what does the loan amortization schedule look like? That's the breakdown of how much interest you will be paying over the life of the proposed loan and provides you an actual dollar amount of how much extra money you must pay back in comparison to what you borrowed. Do not forget this when you refinance! Ask for the loan amortization schedule to understand your true cost.

What is the interest rate?

Mortgage rates, as you know, are always changing. As I write this book, they are an all-time historic low. So why is not everyone rushing out to refinance their mortgage and secure a lower interest rate? Wouldn't that mean that you would be paying less in interest over the life of the loan?

While technically, yes, a lower interest rate does save you on interest over the life of the loan, there are new fees you will incur during the refinance process, which could financially cost you more than your current loan. I've named some them before, and I'll call them out again: an application fee, lender fee, recording fee, appraisal fee, and closing costs to name a few!

You should also consider how much of a lower interest rate you will get when you refinance compared to your current rate. Is the difference 1 percent, 2 percent, or only 0.275 percent? This must be followed by determining how much you currently owe on your mortgage. Obviously, refinancing for a mortgage with an interest rate that is 1 percent less than your current one may make a big difference depending on how large the loan is. Again, it's a simple game of math: What is my real payback on my current loan versus the real payback on the new loan, including factoring in interest and total fees?

Can you shorten the length of the loan?

Most of us got pretty excited when we bought our home and realized we could stretch out our payments over thirty years, thus making the monthly payment more affordable. With the average home purchase price in the U.S. today being $247,000, and hot spot locations like Malibu, California, averaging $3.2 million right now, it's no wonder that 80 percent of homebuyers opted for a fixed-interest thirty-year loan to spread out those payments![18] But thirty years of payments also means thirty years of interest! Why not shorten that time if you possibly can?

I know that a fifteen-year mortgage may not be possible right now for all of us, but it should definitely be the goal. It has far more favorable terms than most thirty-year loans. A fifteen-year loan typically comes with a lower interest rate than longer mortgages, plus, you are cutting the time in half for interest to accrue. thirty years of interest versus fifteen years of interest can save you an insane amount of money:

Thirty-year loan: $500,000 mortgage with a thirty-year term and 3 percent fixed interest rate will cost $758,887 to pay back over the life of the loan.

Fifteen-year loan: $500,000 mortgage with a fifteen-year term and 2.5 percent interest rate (since fifteen years have more favorable interest rates than thirty years) will cost $600,111 to pay back over the life of the loan.

Now, what would switching to a fifteen-year mortgage and seeing savings of $158,776 mean for your family? How could that money enable a dream on your "**If Life Were Perfect** list?

With that kind of savings opportunity, why are we not all rushing out and refinancing our thirty-year mortgage and getting a fifteen-year mortgage instead? Your monthly payment, that's why.

You will unfortunately have a higher monthly payment with a fifteen-year mortgage, since you are having to repay the loan faster than a thirty-year mortgage. For some families, especially in hot spot areas where real estate is through the roof, it's just not possible right now. But with the right goal-setting and planning, you will get there, and should do it the first moment you possibly can.

I promise you that if you stick with paying off your debts like we talked about in this chapter, and you get serious about sticking to your budget as those debts disappear and don't burn out before tackling your mortgage, you will be in a position to eventually switch to a fifteen-year mortgage. And that is a very good goal to have.

In the interim, see if you can secure a more favorable loan than the one you have now (i.e. lower interest rate), as long as you do not opt for a repayment term any longer than what is left on your current mortgage or one that comes with a higher interest rate then what you currently have secured.

Or consider making extra payments on your current loan when you get a bonus or extra cash, assuming your other, more expensive debts have been paid. Some people shorten their mortgage payoff period simply by making extra payments on their current loan. It's important, though, to understand whether it's financially better to refinance your existing loan for a shorter-term loan or make extra payments on your existing loan. That will primarily come down to the interest rate between the two options, since the shorter the loan term, the less interest you'll pay overall. You must also factor in any other fees you may incur from a refinance and talk with a CPA about any tax considerations that we will address under the tax chapter.

I want you to be the family who is mortgage free. I want you to be the family who has a roof over their heads, no matter what. I want you to be the family who lives honestly within their means. And I want you to be the success story of the family who did it!

Get serious about paying off your mortgage, understand the true cost, know your options, and make it happen!

A FINAL THOUGHT ON PAYING OFF YOUR DEBTS

As we now leave the paying off debt chapter behind, I want to leave you with this:

No matter what your situation is right now, no matter how fair or unfair things may be, and no matter what may or may not happen in the future, the only thing that is truly standing between you and becoming debt free is *you*.

I know there are a million reasons you can justifiably point the finger elsewhere, but I would still bet on you having what it takes to overcome your debt any day of the week. I believe you have all you need to put on that helmet, storm that field, and battle through to the endzone. You will win in the end. I know it.

Tell yourself that any time you make a financial decision, any time a financial problem comes, or any time someone or something throws a roadblock in your way, you will get through it and come out stronger. Do not let anyone or anything get between you and a debt-free future.

Now get ready, because it is time to move from the red to black. Let's go and make you some money!

4

INVESTING

WE'VE TALKED A LOT ABOUT how a budget can free up money for better things. But taking control of our spending is only one component of building wealth and securing our family's future. If we really want to attain those things on our **If Life Were Perfect** list, then we must understand *why* and *how* to invest toward them.

When I use the word invest, your mind may go straight to the stock market. And while stocks are a form of an investment, what I want you to hear when I say invest is *water into wine*. If those words made you think *miracle*, then we are in sync.

Investing can be the miracle you need to completely transform your family's finances and future. It can take you from a family who borrows to a family who lends; from a family overworked and underpaid to a family that owns a company; from a family dealing in dimes to one dealing in dollars without lifting your hands. Investing *successfully* can change your life and launch you toward your goals with superspeed.

You don't need to get lucky buying a stock that explodes to experience the miracle of investing. The #1 reason we parents aren't crushing it with investing is that we simply are not doing enough of it. Sure, if we contribute to our company's 401(k) retirement plan, that's investing. We might have an online brokerage account that we throw money into now and then. But beyond those efforts, most of us are not investing, and we're spending way too much money on purchases, expenses, and debts. A dollar spent is not only a dollar lost, but a dollar that can never grow tenfold to build wealth and secure our family's future.

You are already familiar with investing even if you would not describe yourself as an investor. Why? Because if you're like the rest of us, you have invested heavily in credit card companies, car dealerships, student loan institutions, and the bank that owns your home. But in those cases, you were the borrower in those investments rather than the lender. And those companies have made a killing off you. You have paid them so much money over the years in interest that they love you for it. But now that we're becoming wiser and more disciplined when it comes to parting with our money, we're ready to transform ourselves from borrower to lender, and watch all that interest work in our favor as we choose to invest over borrowing and spending.

I want investing to be the miracle that your family's been looking for to help you reach all your goals. If you can stick to your leaner budget, eliminate your debts, and grab all the extra dollars you can, then you'll add miracle maker to your list of titles. It is time for us to invest!

We begin with understanding the rules for investing *successfully*:

1. You must determine how much money you will need to reach your **If Life Were Perfect** goals.

Starting with the end in mind dictates every move we make going forward. How much money are those goals going to cost?

Landing on an answer will require you to get a little more goal-specific. For example, if you wrote down on your **If Life Were Perfect** list that you want to pay for your children's college, take that goal even further and write down what that really means to you. Are we talking private college paying top dollar or a state school that's less expensive? Or if you wrote down retire early, are we talking about retirement in a modest Midwestern town or somewhere like Manhattan? That's what determines the cost.

Most of us are not sure exactly how much money we will need for our larger long-term goals like retirement, health costs, lifestyle costs, and necessary principle for our family nest egg. We will talk in the Players section about how a financial advisor can help you determine those numbers, but they will need to know your goals!

2. You must identify how much time you have between now and funding your goals.

Once you know how much money each goal requires, then you must determine how much time you want to spend reaching them. Timing is a major factor when it comes to the investment strategies you'll use. Most financial experts say five years and beyond is the common benchmark for what's considered a long-term investment.

For example, if your child starts college in two years, then you will probably want any college savings account for your child invested more conservatively, so the value of the account won't nosedive if the market tanks right as your kid needs the money for college. But if your child starts college in ten years, then we can invest more aggressively because we have more time to ride out a dip in the market or a decrease in the value of the college savings account.

Obviously, the earlier you can start investing before you need to reach a goal, the more investment strategies you can choose from and the more time you'll have to ride out the market's natural ups and downs: inflation, interest rates, economic growth, unemployment rates, wars, and pandemics. They will all contribute to the returns we can expect during our investment journey. Investing earlier also means the longer that interest can compound on our investments and produce those bigger returns. For example, investing $200 per month beginning at age thirty-five with a 7 percent return will provide you more than *double* what you will have by age sixty-five than if you wait to begin contributing at age forty-five.[19]

Even investments outside the markets are more successful with time. The sooner you invest in your education, acquire more knowledge, or learn a new skill, the sooner you are increasing your earning potential, resulting in more money over time. The sooner you invest in real estate, the more time you can collect rent from tenants and the property can gain in value. The sooner you start a successful business, the longer you can grow it and reach more paying customers.

That said, please don't get discouraged just because you didn't buy stock when you were ten years old or start a business your senior year of high school. Contrary to popular belief, research published in the *Harvard Business Review* found that the average age of a successful startup founder is age forty-five![20] We should not feel like the best years are behind us to jump in the game right now! The key is to get started now and keep time on your side.

3. You must not invest more than you can afford to lose.

Just as an investment can be the miracle to superspeed you toward reaching your **If Life Were Perfect** goals, it can also be a death sentence if the investment fails.

Too many families make the mistake of investing money they simply cannot afford to lose. While I want to help you do whatever it takes to scrounge up money to invest, it must not be money you need to pay those bills today in your leaner budget or money you know you'll need to access in the near future.

We usually hear about this rule—don't invest money you can't afford to lose—when it comes to older people who need money for retirement and mistakenly leave their money invested too aggressively. Then, BANG! A recession hits right before they retire. That was money they needed to have and to access for basic living needs; continuing to invest it aggressively was too risky. The money tied up in their investment became money they simply could not afford to lose.

There are also families who pull equity out of their home, or borrow money from their emergency fund, or money earmarked for basic living needs, and invest it, only to lose everything when the investment does not pan out. I will never forget a friend's family having to move out of their ritzy harbor home and over-hearing the parents discussing how the dad's real estate investments had failed.

You need to get in the game of investing with every possible dollar to spare. But do not invest money (or invest too aggressively) you simply cannot afford to lose!

4. You must understand your risk tolerance.

Before you determine your investment strategies, you need to assess your personality and your attitude toward taking risks. Just because you like to skydive does not mean you like risk with your finances! You can take two people who are the exact same age, have the exact same amount of money, and have the exact same **If Life Were Perfect** list, and find that investing excites one and ter-rifies the other.

All investments come with the risk of losing money. Some investments are characterized as more conservative, meaning the priority is to preserve your investment as much as possible even if that means smaller returns. Aggressive investments, on the other hand, prioritize higher returns over preserving the initial investment. Aggressive investments are riskier, with preservation not being a top priority. And they require the investor to have a higher personal tolerance for taking risk.

Most financial experts will tell you that the best way to mitigate risk in general, whether for a conservative or an aggressive investment, is to do your homework first and then carefully estimate the likely outcome. What truly makes an investment risky is not understanding the actual risk! If we are not willing to take *some* risk whether for a conservative or aggressive investment, we simply will not increase our money and thus reach our goals on our **If Life Were Perfect** list. Only you can decide what your ultimate goals are for your family, but I urge all of us to understand the role that risk must play in that journey.

5. You must diversify your investments.

Putting your eggs all in one basket—or nest—can be wonderful if those eggs all hatch. But if anything happens to that nest and those eggs, you've lost everything. That's why smart investors understand the need to diversify their investments.

The Walt Disney Company is a great example of an investor who understands this concept. The company diversified their investments by expanding beyond their core animation business into theme parks, cruise lines, hotels and resorts, live entertainment, residential communities, television, and more. While the Walt Disney Company took a terrible hit during the pandemic as people could not visit their parks or watch their movies in theaters, they reported explosive growth with their live streaming services as people were home watching shows.[21] That's how diversification works. When one venture tanks, you still have other ones to rely on that could be making a profit and carrying you toward your goals.

I see this work with everyday families. They've built wealth in a variety of ways through a collection of different investment strategies. When the stock market is volatile, their bond investments usually hold steady. When their business they own is slow, they still enjoy income from their real estate investments. Most of us will need to diversify our investments to reach our **If Life Were Perfect** goals.

6. You must keep up with inflation!

Have you ever heard the expression that if you aren't moving forward, you are moving backward? Well, that applies to our money as well! If you keep all your extra money in a regular savings account year after year, you're actually losing money over the long-term. Why? Because of inflation.

Inflation is the rate at which the general level of prices for goods and services rises and, consequently, the purchasing power of your dollar falls. The dollar I had sitting on my dresser a year ago had more value in the marketplace than it does today because the cost of living has since increased.

I had a client who had more than a million dollars sitting in a regular savings account. When I asked her what that was all about, she said she saved it to pay cash for a home and had yet to find one she wanted. My jaw almost dropped! First, how incredible at her relatively young age to have saved a million dollars cash, and two, how incredible that she had no idea how inflation works! At a minimum, that money she saved should have been in an interest-bearing savings account to keep up with the cost of inflation.

With the cost of inflation as I write this book sitting at 2 percent per year, every dollar that's not accruing at least 2 percent interest each year is losing its value.[22] For all you awesome savers out there, remember the cost of inflation!

Now that you understand the basic rules of investing, it is time to look at your different investment options. Because you have your **If Life Were Perfect** list and understand the rules and yourself better, you can choose what makes sense for you.

INVESTING IN YOURSELF

Warren Buffet, one of the world's richest people, a man known for smart investments, said "ultimately, there's one investment that supersedes all others: Invest in yourself. Nobody can take away what you've got in yourself, and everybody has potential they haven't used yet."[23]

Everyday parents like you and me, even those experiencing tremendous financial hardship or life challenges, can rise to the occasion and change our finances, our families, and our futures, by investing in ourselves. For some, that means going back to school to finish their degree, knowing it can open new doors. For others, that means learning a new skill that makes them more valuable to their company or helps them get promoted. For still others, it means taking a course on technology or public speaking so they can have a bigger voice in the world. Think of the ways you could invest in yourself right now that would lead to making you more dollars.

My client Melinda came to understand this concept when she was facing great financial hardship. Her beautiful daughter was born with severe special needs and Melinda had to quit her job to be there for her as she was constantly in and out of the Pediatric Intensive Care Unit for years. It was impossible for Melinda to hold a nine-to-five job. The loss of income sent her family in a downward financial spiral. After Melinda's husband suddenly left, Melinda knew she had to find a way to provide for her disabled, medically fragile daughter and her other young daughter.

That's when the owner of the Home Health Agency, which provided government subsidized part-time nursing care for Melinda's daughter, encouraged Melinda to become a nurse. She wanted to hire Melinda and pay her to care for her own daughter. She knew Melinda had extensive experience, not just caring for her own disabled daughter, but providing care for others. Meanwhile, a nurse from the Home Health Agency encouraged Melinda to go to school and said she would work her hours caring for Melinda's daughter while Melinda was in class. (How great is that to hear how these women supported Melinda!)

Melinda knew that going back to school would be difficult. She hadn't set foot in classroom since graduating high school more than thirty-five years ago. When she took the admissions test, the Director of Nurses from the part-time nursing program looked at her test results with her and said, "Well, I've seen worse. You're going to need to work harder. But, because you have so much real-life experience caring for others and your own daughter, we have a spot for you in our program if you'd like to attend." That moment alone felt like a big door opening right before her eyes.

Through student loans, financial aid, and the help and encouragement of others, Melinda worked hard in the program and maintained As and Bs. She graduated with almost an A average and became a nurse and was hired by the Home Health Agency. Melinda now gets paid to care for her daughter and be there for her, while simultaneously financially providing for her family.

Had Melinda not had the courage to go back to school and invest in herself, she would have lost out on substantial income and the opportunity to continue caring for her daughter. Melinda saw the investment she made in herself and her family as nothing short of the miracle her family needed to survive. She concluded her remarkable story by saying "Can you believe it? I became a nurse and I get paid to care for my daughter. God has been so good to me."

If we were looking at your finances together right now, regardless of whether you are struggling with debt or have extra money to invest, how could investing in yourself help grow your finances and secure your family's future? What skill could you learn to become more of an expert in your field? What license could you get to help you secure a better paying job? What book could you read or podcast could you listen to that would help you increase your knowledge? You are investing in yourself just by reading this book!

Don't leave all those missed opportunity dollars on the table by failing to invest in yourself. And in case you were second doubting yourself, yes, you are well worth the investment.

INVESTING IN THE MARKET

I met James* and Allison* when they asked me for help getting their finances and estate plan in order. My assistant noted the meeting was urgent, and when I read their intake form, I saw that James owned stock in a start-up tech company that had skyrocketed. James's stock had recently been valued at $20 million. Then I understood why he wrote *retired* as his employment status: retired at the ripe old age of forty-five!

Not all of us will hit the jackpot like James when it comes to owning stock or investing in the market. But the good news is that, historically, even conservative investments increase in value over time. Records show that, since its inception in 1928, the stock market has an average return of 10 percent annually.[24]

Investing your money in the financial market is basically investing in other people. You are investing in someone else's company or in someone else's debt. It's probably the most common way people grow their money without the lifting of their own hands. It is the traditional way your money grows in retirement and brokerage accounts.

There are different methods to grow your money when you invest it in the market. I'm going to familiarize you with the most common options—stocks, bonds, mutual funds and exchange traded funds (ETFs), and annuities—so you have a general understanding of how they work. I can't give you specific advice on what is best for you, but I will give you some things to think about and how to go about it all.

Stocks

Buying an individual stock means you are buying partial ownership in someone else's company. Because you have partial ownership, you get to share in that company's profits and losses. The good news, again, is that historically stocks have increased in value over time, meaning the dollar you put in today becomes multiple dollars you get in return down the road. Investing in stocks for our age group as parents of non-adult children makes a lot of sense, since we have time on our side to ride the natural ups and downs of the market before we need to access those funds for retirement.

When you are investing in someone else's company, like buying a stock, it is important to understand the way you can make money. There are a variety of companies to invest in—from established companies who will pay you dividends (income) while you own the stock without a high probability that the stock itself will explode, to growing companies who will pay little or no dividends but with higher probability the stock itself will increase in value, to start-up companies whose success is extremely difficult to predict and with whom there's risk of losing everything or making ridiculous gains if the company takes off (like in my client James's case).

You must understand what type of stock you are purchasing and everything you can about the company. *Who are you dealing with? What do the experts predict for growth? What are your likely dividends, what is the potential for the stock to skyrocket or nosedive, and what are the companies' risks? What are your risks, as well? Do you have the money and the time you need to see this investment through?* While no one can ever consistently predict what will happen in the market or for any company, doing your research and sticking to the rules we talked about before can help you evaluate wisely.

Bonds

Bonds are basically where you lend money to a company or government entity and then charge them interest until they pay you back (the time for repayment is established when you loan the money). The company or government entity makes interest payments to you along the way, and then returns the original amount borrowed from you at the end. It's kind of like being a credit card company where you're the lender, and having the company or government entity borrow from you (except that the repayment time is established, and interest does not compound). You can also sell the bond to someone else if you want out of the deal (assuming its attractive for someone to buy it).

Like any investment, bonds have their pros and cons. The upshot is that bonds are fairly conservative investments and might be more attractive when stocks are volatile. Rather than betting on a company's growth like you do with stocks, you are instead betting on a company being able to repay their debt.

The downside is that the Federal Reserve may subsequently raise interest rates during the term of your existing bond, making new bonds more attractive to buy. Who is going to want to buy your bond with its lower interest rate when they could buy a new bond with a higher interest rate? You may get stuck with a bond getting a lower return than what you could by getting in today's market. This is called interest rate risk.

There are other risks beyond a rising interest rate that can affect the value of the bond. What if the company or government entity

THE FAMILY NEST EGG

repays it early or defaults on the loan? Taking time to understand the pros and cons of any investment, given your unique profile as an investor (age, time, risk tolerance, need, etc.) will help you make smart choices.

Mutual Funds and ETFs

A mutual fund and ETF are basically collections of different stocks or bonds, and you and other investors each have partial ownership in that mutual fund or ETF. Think of it as a group of your friends all going in together on different lotto tickets and agreeing to split the costs, the losses, and the winnings. (Don't worry, stocks or bonds have much better odds than the lottery!)

The stocks or bonds chosen could be diverse, or for similar companies (i.e. companies with growth potential). Someone called a portfolio manager, whom you pay, will choose the stocks or bonds to include and manage the mutual fund or ETF for your group. The appeal of the mutual fund or ETF is that an investor can get broad diversification with a small investment, especially if you can't afford to buy your own basket of individual stocks.

People tend to like mutual funds or ETFs because they see it as diverse, and they can buy into many different investments for a small amount of money. Rather than betting it all on one single stock, with a mutual fund or ETF there are multiple stocks or bonds. You as a group share in the wins and losses collectively.

Annuities

An annuity is a contract between you and an insurance company where you pay a lump sum of money up front to the insurance company, and they agree to pay you a regular income either starting immediately or later. This is different than a life insurance policy that comes with a death benefit.

The goal of an annuity is to provide you a steady stream of income, typically during your retirement years. So, if we bought an annuity today and did not want to get paid until we retire, that's a lot of years for our lump sum investment to grow before you start getting payments.

There are two main types of annuities: qualified or non-qualified. Qualified annuities are funded with pre-tax dollars (similar to your 401(k)) but the payments you receive from the annuity are subject to income tax since you did not pay taxes on the contributions or growth. Non-qualified annuities, however, are funded with post-tax dollars, and you will only owe taxes on a portion of the payments you receive from the annuity because you already paid some taxes.

Annuities also come with different guarantees, like the minimum rate of return you will get or a guaranteed interest rate.

People like annuities because they seem conservative and straightforward, but there are actually many nuances, and they can be incredibly expensive when you factor in the fees or if you need to get out of your contract to access money early. That's why it's so important to understand the true cost of this investment.

Now that we've talked about stocks, mutual funds and ETFs, bonds, and annuities, I am guessing your take away is that there are a lot of pros and cons for each different strategy, and a lot depends on your goals, your age, your time in the market, your risk tolerance, and need to diversify. This is why people hire professionals who study this all day long and help you make these evaluations and decisions. You will hear me talk a lot in the Players section about how a professional financial advisor can help you.

STARTING A BUSINESS

Starting your own business can be one of the greatest investments you can make. The self-respect that comes with building something from nothing alone is incredibly worthwhile.

Many people love the idea of leaving their nine-to-five job, making their own hours, being their own boss, and not having their income capped by a salary like it is when they are employed by someone else's company. But while many people dream of starting their own business, statistically 90 percent of businesses will fail.[25]

There are many reasons a business fails but, surprisingly, a challenging economy is not one of them. Look no further than Thomas Edison, the Disney Brothers, Bill Gates, Steve Jobs, Jeff Bezos, Elon Musk, and Mark Zuckerberg, all of whom experienced tremendous financial gains from their companies during troubled economic times![26] That's why Warren Buffet says he evaluates where to invest based on a company's probable success rather than the economy itself.

So, why do so many businesses fail, and how can you be sure the one you want to start or already have started will not be one of them? Most businesses fail because of a lack of funding, lack of management, poor infrastructure or business model, bad marketing, or the business owner calling it quits.[27]

But when a business is correctly structured and succeeds, the financial and personal benefits are incredible. Many of my clients own successful businesses—from a small accounting firm, to a national marketing company, to a worldwide restaurant chain. While their types of business and size may vary, they all had common core indicators that their businesses would succeed and enable the personal lifestyles they wanted. Once you understand these core indicators, then you can evaluate if owning your own business will be an incredible investment for you.

Here are the five common core indicators of whether a business will succeed:

1. The business is well funded.

It takes money to make money, and that is the case for any start-up business. Not only do most business owners not initially make a profit, they also spend a lot of money to make it launch. If a business does not have the right capital or funding, the business will not make it. I told you earlier about how a lack of funding almost financially crushed my husband and me when we first started our law firm, and how we had to quickly take control of our finances to ensure our family and business would succeed. Talk about sleepless nights!

Even after a business launches and becomes more well-established, it will continue to face cash flow issues. I think of the multi-million-dollar company I advised who listed "cash flow" as their number one challenge. All businesses must regularly review their personal and business cash flow so there are proper financial reserves and continual capital to keep operating. How many companies did you personally see close their doors within the first two weeks of the pandemic? They did not have enough funding and capital to sustain their operations and weather that unexpected storm.

How do you know how much money it will take to see your business succeed? Having a business plan with necessary expenses can help you grasp all that operating your business will financially require. And having a close relationship each month with your numbers, along with a proper reserve, can ensure your business can continue even in less profitable months.

People fund their businesses in many ways, including from their own pocket, a loan, other investors, or from family or friends. But no matter where the funding may come from, the business owner ultimately must pay it back. Like any investment you make, you should not invest more than you can afford to lose and when there is not a well-calculated probability of return.

2. The business is properly staffed.

Having a successful business will require putting together the right team. Think of your team like a puzzle. You need all the pieces, and they all have to fit. A lack of staff or high turnover is a huge disruption to a business and has caused many of them to fail. They say the reason businesses like Costco are so profitable is because of a low staff turnover, helping them avoid the 30 percent to 50 percent cost of the employee's annual salary it takes to go through the process of replacing them if they leave.[28]

Many businesses initially begin with just the owner, and their blood, sweat, and tears. But if your business is only you, that is not really a business yet! I think of my friend with a very profitable firm who worked most of our shared vacation because he did not have a team to cover in his absence. While my husband and I were getting texts from our team back home with new business closed, our friend was tied to his laptop, stressed out, and overwhelmed, even though he was making great money! The true success of a business is when its owner can step away and have the business continue without them. Without a team, a business owner is simply self-employed.

Even businesses who have a team must have the proper training and roles for the business to succeed. There's a great restaurant in town that is closing its doors even though it has many employees and is profitable. The owner did not build her team correctly or properly train them to run things in her absence. Now that her husband's health is failing, she has decided to close the doors to a business that should have continued to run without her while also providing her an income.

Business owners understand that, ultimately, they must wear the business-owner hat and not the employee hat. The business owner cannot continually be working *in* their business, but evolve to only working *on* it. Having the right team in place is key for any business's success.

3. The business has a great infrastructure and business model.

Systems, systems, and systems. Without them you are rolling the dice, blindly betting that your product and service will consistently deliver the same results to every paying customer. Too many companies do not invest in the right infrastructure to make their business succeed. Too much remains floating in the owner or staff members' heads when it needs to be down on paper and part of an overall system. What happens if the owner or a key employee misses a day of work or leaves early? Not delivering a consistent product or client experience can lead to disappointed customers and a business closing its doors.

Another major consideration that you would think business owners would address beforehand is how they plan to make money. Their business model itself must be well-thought-out and profit-able. Too many businesses randomly charge for an item or service without first understanding how much money it will cost them to provide that item or service, and then how much money they must charge for the business to make a sustainable profit. If a business is not making a profit, it will obviously fail!

For these reasons, franchises are usually incredibly attractive. A franchise business owner can purchase rights to open a location from a large chain and have access to their tried and true

business model, name recognition, infrastructure, and reputation. Unlike starting something from scratch, a franchise has
already figured out the secret to making their business profitable and you—as the franchise owner—are simply replicating
it. While you can certainly create your own infrastructure and
business model from scratch for your own business, you must
understand the business model and infrastructure you need to
make it work.

4. The business can attract paying customers.

Think of a product or service that you use in your everyday life.
Why did you choose to buy that product or use that service over
a competitor's? While you might say it is because you like their
product or service better, you would have never known that unless
having first discovered the product or service you like in the first
place. That is where effective marketing comes in.

Marketing is a company's way of getting their message out and
converting paying customers. It's more necessary than ever in a
world with so much competition. You can literally buy a product
or use a service from anywhere in the world. While we may stop
by the local market because it is close by and convenient, even that
was a calculated marketing decision by management to put the
store where they knew you would see it because they wanted
people like you to shop there.

Do you remember the George Foreman grill? It was that indoor
grill that legendary boxer George Foreman marketed with over
100 million sold worldwide! What is interesting is that the grill
itself was invented by a regular guy named Michael W. Boehm
who had little success selling his grill until George Foreman came
along and they built a massive marketing campaign around him.
That is the power of great marketing.

Business owners must continually ask themselves: how can we make people aware we exist, and what can we do to attract them? From running social media ads, to asking for online reviews, to plastering specials across store windows, to hoping happy customers will tell their friends, your business must have a continuous marketing plan to attract paying customers in a rapidly changing environment.

5. The business owner understands what it takes to run the business.

The most important consideration every business owner must honestly think through is whether they want to own a business and are willing to see it through. I've personally seen too many business owners throw in the towel, even when the business itself is profitable. I can tell you firsthand that owning a business is not easy.

When you own a business, especially when it is in its infancy, you are investing far more than just your hard-earned money. You are investing your time, your energy, your resources, and even your personal reputation. You are tasked with making decisions on everything from what product or service you are offering, to what legal contracts get signed, to who takes out the trash. You deal with the wins and the losses and all the inherent problems that will arise, like an unhappy client or a disruption to production. And most significantly, you have your employees relying on you to feed their families. Will you honor that responsibility and have the grit to see your business through?

Owning a business requires a realistic assessment of what it will personally cost you to run it beyond just the money you invest. Owning a business must help facilitate, and not sabotage, those things you want most on your **If Life Were Perfect** list. Sure, you will have times when you are busier than others, but if your business continually disrupts your personal life, something will have to give. I will never forget the business owner of a very profitable company who could not understand why his adult son was still angry with him for missing his youth sports events and for divorcing his mother. All that success in his business, only to have his family fail. No financial investment is ever worth it if it costs you what matters most.

Now that you understand the core indicators of a successful business, you can decide if starting a business or continuing the one you have is the right decision for you. If you decide it's a jump you want to take, I hope it turns out to be one of the best life changing decisions you have ever made and I can't wait to follow your success!

INVESTING IN REAL ESTATE

Ryan* is a real estate investor I helped to set up his legal and estate planning, and to protect his assets from any potential lawsuits. He was not even thirty years old and already owned a company connected to a popular television show where he and his partner would secure funding from outside investors, buy distressed properties, remodel them, and then sell them. He made a killing off his investments in real estate.

Like investing in yourself, the financial market, and your own business, investing in real estate is another strategy for turning *water into wine*. You can purchase a rental property, like a single-family home, a condo, a duplex, a high rise, a commercial building, or undeveloped land and rent it out to receive steady monthly income on an asset that will historically rise in value over time. Notice what type of property I excluded—your personal residence. And that's because while your home certainly may increase in value, there are other considerations for buying a personal residence than when you buy investment properties.

You don't necessarily have to be a professional real estate investor or a tv show host to reap the benefits that come from investing in real estate. Many of my clients who are lawyers, doctors, or have any number of normal day jobs, invest in real estate to diversify their investments and have a monthly income, especially during their retirement years.

My business-owning clients often buy a commercial property and then rent it back to their business, rather than pay rent to someone else. The business then has a place to operate, and the business owner now owns a building and land that will historically increase in value. If their building has additional space that their business is not using or if they outgrow their space, they can always rent it to other tenants and receive monthly rental income.

There are also tremendous tax benefits that come from real estate investing, as you can typically depreciate the costs of the building each year—which helps offset the taxes you must pay on the rent you collect.

Real estate investors are attracted to this form of investing primarily because of how you can finance property. The idea is that you secure a loan by only putting 20 percent down, and then rent out the property and have someone else pay the mortgage through their rental payments, for an asset that will ultimately be yours. Some of my investor clients do not even use their own money to fund their real estate investments, but instead gather a group of investors who provide the capital and purchase a property together, then share in the rents or proceeds when it's sold with the main investor taking a nice cut.

So why are we not all jumping in the real estate investment game? The primary reason is that unlike other investments that seem more common and known, real estate seems foreign for many people. They don't understand how the investment works or don't have the desire or ability to put in the time to learn how to do it. We've also all heard horror stories that are unfortunately true. I'll tell you about my tenant who turned my rental into a drug house another time!

As you think about whether you'd want to jump in this game, consider these important questions: *Do you want to spend time studying the real estate market and finding a property that will likely produce a return? Do you want to spend time doing the analysis of your potential cash flow during ownership? Do you want to be a landlord and be responsible for ongoing maintenance and repairs? Do you want to kick a family out if they fail to pay their rent? Can you afford to cover a vacancy or all the inherent property ownership costs? Do you want to deal with legalities like housing laws and asset protection?* While you can certainly get professionals to help you handle these things, you are ultimately responsible and must understand the full deal.

Another huge consideration is whether you can afford to have your money tied up in real estate. Real estate is typically a long-term play and too many of my clients are property rich but cash poor. Sure, there are quicker real estate deals—like flipping—but those are the riskiest, as you cannot predict the market. That's what happened in 2009, when so many investors lost their investment properties when the real estate market tanked before they could sell.

If you like the idea of investing in real estate but wish to do so more from a distance, buying into a real estate investment trust (REIT) could be a great option for you. This allows you to invest in a company that owns and operates real estate properties. They handle the dirty work, and you reap the rewards and can usually get out of them fairly quickly, unlike when you own a property.

Be sure when you go to diversify your investments, you do not overlook the benefits that can come from owning real estate!

A FINAL THOUGHT ON INVESTING

We're going to move on to funding important life milestones, which will obviously require money. My question for you is, are you going to stay where you are right now, or start investing in your future?

Ten years ago, I sat at a kitchen table, wondering if I had made the biggest mistake of my life when I decided to invest in myself and my own business by opening a law firm. Before that, I had been made the lead attorney for a California city by the age of twenty-six, only to end up completely switching practice fields to finance and estate planning and having to learn a whole new area of law. I felt like I had gone from being so far ahead of the pack to having to start again. I saw my friends rising at law firms—even making partner!—when I was now making my own marketing flyers.

But what I've learned is that our past wins and losses can all come together to be used for our good. Nothing that's happened in your past can't be somehow used for your great future. Don't be afraid to get off the bench and try something new on the field. Don't be afraid to go for that deep pass or even the Hail Mary! Don't be afraid to invest in yourself, even if it requires big change. Don't think the best years are behind you, but know they are right now and in front of you.

I know that you have everything it takes to experience the miracle of investing. I saw this happen for my own family, and I know it can happen for yours, too.

5

FUNDING LIFE
MILESTONES

ARE YOU READY TO HIT your life milestones? I'm talking about four big ones—homebuying, funding your kids' college educations, taking vacations and organizing special occasions, and retirement. And let's hit those other goals on your **If Life Were Perfect** list, too, while we're at it!

Are you excited to stick to your leaner budget, eliminate your debt, and experience the miracle of investing?

How would you like to live in that neighborhood you've had your eye on and say goodbye to your landlord or the home you've outgrown?

How would you like to send your child off to college knowing it won't break your bank account or saddle them with debt?

How would you like to finally take a well-deserved vacation?

And how would you like to live, knowing that your final years will truly be golden because of smart choices you are making today?

I'm not suggesting that you have to live extravagantly to be happy or that you've got to write a check for all these life milestones tomorrow. No, this is where smart and practical planning comes in. But I think you're going to be thrilled knowing that the choices you make today will secure your tomorrow, allowing you to comfortably enjoy important life milestones free of anxiety or struggle.

BUYING A FAMILY HOME

Buying a family home is a big milestone many families hope to reach. I would guess that some of you have hit this important milestone already, and that's why we talked about paying off your mortgage back in the debt section.

Yet, for far too many of us parents, especially those of us living in big cities and affluent areas where homes are extraordinarily expensive, we have yet to hit this big milestone (or we want to hit it again). It may feel impossible at times.

Homes are expensive! The average home cost in the United States, as of this writing, is $320,000, with homes costing less in the Midwest, but much more in places like Manhattan or Los Angeles, where homes typically cost in the millions! Many families renting in these expensive areas are struggling to save up for a down payment on a home, not to mention the cash to pay for the full purchase price! I know this from firsthand experience as my husband and I had to save up for a down payment to buy a home in Newport Beach, California, where the average home price is a whopping 2.3 million dollars!

I know there are many financial and personal barriers that have made buying a home challenging for you. If you're a Gen X parent, you lived through the 2009 financial crisis when people you knew lost their homes, and maybe you did too. You'll recall that lenders were qualifying buyers for homes they could not really afford through subprime mortgages that came with an adjustable interest rate. As the interest rate rose, increasing borrowers' payments, the values of homes were simultaneously decreasing. When families could no longer afford their higher monthly payments, and home values simultaneously dropped, homeowners could not refinance or sell—and the banks ultimately foreclosed. How many of us parents experienced that nightmare and have hesitated to jump back in the housing game?

I also know that for you Millennial parents, while you largely avoided the mortgage crisis because you were on the younger side, your barrier to home ownership has been your large student loan payments and high cost of rent, making it difficult to save for a down payment.[29] For better or worse, there are much stricter requirements now for you to qualify for a mortgage loan due to lending reforms made after the housing crisis.

I also know some of you simply cannot afford to buy where you wish to live. You look at the home prices, then you look at your budget, and there seems to be a huge gap. I know my husband and I certainly felt that way when went to buy our home here in California. While, yes, you should consider buying in a less expensive area, and you know many families who did that and made very happy lives for themselves, I understand that moving elsewhere from where you wish to live is neither ideal nor always practical.

Maybe you want to live near your family, your job, or your favorite lifestyle venues, which happens to be expensive! Only *you* can set the goals for your family and only *you* know what is best. Just remember that the homebuying milestone may get delayed until you can close that gap between your available cash, your budget, and those home prices, which means sticking with a leaner budget while increasing your income, possibly through major changes and smart investments. For Josh and me, leaving our day jobs and starting our own business while sticking to a leaner budget led to greater financial returns that made homebuying possible for us. But it required sacrifice and did not happen overnight. You will know what changes you must make, too.

I know that if you stick with the Three Ps—Plan, Protect, and Players—homebuying will be possible for you. Let's see some checklist points you have to consider before reaching this special milestone:

1. You *want* to own a home.

Most of us parents immediately turn to questions like *Can I afford to buy a home?* or *Where would I want to live?* or *Is buying this home a good financial investment?* instead of taking a step back and asking if we want to be homeowners in the first place.

For many of us, it's incredibly important to own a home so we can do what we want with our living space, like remodel or paint the kitchen the color we want. Some of us want to know that the money we're paying each month is going toward something we will own, as opposed to a rental arrangement. And some of us feel like owning a home is *officially* laying down roots or a big personal accomplishment.

But not everyone wants to own a home. You may want to keep your options open for moving in a year or two, or maybe you just relocated and want to get a feel of the different neighborhoods around you, or maybe you had a big life change like a divorce or remarriage and you want your new normal to settle in more before laying down roots. Some of us like renting because we have just a fantastic deal or we like not having to deal with home ownership costs like broken pipes.

It's important for you to be honest with yourself about what homeownerships means to you. It's also important to understand what homeownership means to your spouse so that you both agree it fits within your goals, circumstances, and budget.

2. It's the right time to buy a home.

How many parents do you know who can afford to buy a home but are waiting for the *right time* to buy a home? I equate this to waiting for the perfect spouse or waiting for the perfect time to have a baby. It just doesn't work like that.

My client Pete* is a prime example of this trap. He and his wife did the hard part of saving up for a down payment but were afraid to buy because Pete had lost his first home during the 2009 mortgage crisis. Once he financially recovered, he's been renting ever since, waiting year after year to buy, convinced the housing market will slide again and that this time he won't be its victim. The problem is that Pete has now spent ten years paying rent waiting to scoop up a property only after its value has hit rock bottom, yet our current market remains steady at an all-time high.

Too many of us parents are like Pete, understandably waiting for something to happen that makes homebuying more attractive or safe, especially if we have been burned before. The problem is that we absolutely cannot control outside factors like housing prices going down, or housing inventory going up, or the economy changing, or an election being over. How many of you like Pete have been waiting for optimal circumstances to come along for years? While there is always a prime time in the market to buy a home, you would only know what it was using hindsight. You simply cannot time the market.

Financial experts agree that it is less about *timing* the market, and more about *time in* the market when it comes to building wealth. The sooner you jump in the game, the sooner you stop paying rent, the sooner you begin building equity in a home, the sooner you can pay off your mortgage.

3. You can afford the down payment.

Coming up with a down payment—the percentage of the full purchase price you must front to secure a mortgage loan—is one of the major obstacles to home ownership.

The biggest mistake I see families make is assuming they cannot afford to buy a home because they don't understand their options for a mortgage loan. Not all mortgage loans are the same! Just because it's common to put 20 percent down on a home, parents erroneously assume that's their only financing option. Or they may not understand that if they do not put at least 20 percent down, they will have to pay private mortgage insurance that gets built into their mortgage until they reach 20 percent equity in their home (through paying down the mortgage or the home value rising). Or they mistakenly believe that because they are a first-time homebuyer, they will automatically qualify for Federal Housing Association (FHA) loan through a government program, without realizing the loan amount is limited. It's so important to educate yourself about the loan options available to you and which one can make homebuying possible for you.

Once you know your loan options and terms, then you can look back at your budget and see how they align. Many families unfortunately find themselves falling short. You hear of parents who borrow the down payment from a relative or borrow money from themselves (through their retirement accounts). Candidly, if you have to borrow money for a down payment and must pay that back in addition to your mortgage, lender fees, closing costs, moving costs, and home improvement needs, then you probably are not ready to buy a home. Also know your lender will require you to have a certain amount of financial reserves left in your accounts after you close on the loan. This means you cannot deplete your accounts for the down payment.

This may leave you going back, once again, to your budget and seeing where you can find the money. Go back through every line item expense and ask, is this more important to me than buying a home? You will be surprised at the extra dollars you will find when you approach your budget with this mentality. Also go back to see if there is any possible way to increase your income through the investment strategies we talked about, like getting a better job, asking for raise, using a bonus, starting a side hustle or a business, and whatever else you can think of! I know families who have temporarily moved in with parents or rented a smaller apartment for a year or two while they saved up for the down payment. It may not be ideal, but in the grand scheme of things it becomes a minor blip that enables them to get into the housing game.

Do not get discouraged. If you stick with your leaner budget and implement the other techniques in this book, I promise you it will only be a matter of time before you come up with that down payment.

4. You can afford the monthly payments on a fixed-rate mortgage.

Some financial experts argue that you should only pay cash for a home. Others argue you should finance your home and invest your cash elsewhere for a higher return. Others say to only take out a fifteen-year mortgage or less (which we talked extensively about in Chapter Three). How do you know what makes the most sense for your family?

The reality is that very few families, especially those in expensive areas, can pay all-cash for a home or afford a fifteen-year mortgage. That's why 80 percent of homeowners have a thirty-year fixed rate mortgage, allowing them to spread their payments out over time and providing them a lower monthly mortgage payment. Thirty years, of course, means a much longer time period for interest to apply, and it will cost you far more to pay back in the end compared to a fifteen-year loan. (Remember to avoid adjustable mortgages in low interest rate environments like the one at the time of this writing.) The moment you can refinance to a fifteen-year mortgage, you can start saving a lot on interest.

Only you can look at your budget and know what is realistic. Whatever loan term you choose, the question remains, can you *afford* that monthly mortgage payment—"afford" meaning, can you cover the monthly mortgage payment in addition to comfortably meeting your other financial responsibilities? The good news is that lenders will not allow you to get a mortgage anymore if your debt ratio to your income is too high, and possibly even if your credit score is too poor. Really look at your budget to make sure you can afford the monthly payment and still enjoy a high quality of life and continue to work toward achieving your other financial goals.

5. You can be in the home at least ten years.

If money is tight getting into a property and you are opting for a thirty-year fixed rate mortgage because you need lower payments, you will want to make sure your family can comfortably live in that home for at least ten years. That way you can ride out the natural housing market cycle with highs and lows, and presumably sell the home for more than you originally paid, covering the cost of your past mortgage payments and any upfront purchase costs you incurred. If you can't stay in the property long enough to cover those costs, you are taking a serious risk that you will lose money on your home purchase or be stuck in a home that does not work for your family.

6. The home you found is where you want to be quarantined.

We would never have considered this until the pandemic hit. How many of us walked around our home the first week of the pandemic and felt happy that this place was *home*. Or how many us, unfortunately, felt the opposite? How many of us looked at our neighborhood differently? How many of us rethought our entire lifestyle and what was most important? How many of us felt sad living so far away from our family and knowing we could not easily travel to see them?

If the pandemic had a positive side, it might have been seeing our lives through new lenses. Maybe our small high-rise condo lost its appeal and we longed for a home with some land. Or maybe we loved that small high-rise condo even more because it was close by our friends or family. Write down on your **If Life Were Perfect** list what you want most in a home, where it would be, who would be near, what would your neighborhood be like, how would the schools be, and how you would feel. Use that as your guide and the right home will come along.

And once you do find that perfect home you love, and you are in the right position to buy, don't be afraid to go for it and make that house your home! I wish you the happiest of family-home memories to come.

PAYING FOR YOUR KIDS' HIGHER EDUCATION

In an ideal world, we could send our kids to the best colleges possible and money would grow on trees to pay for it. With the average cost of tuition and fees for the 2019-2020 school year at $41,426 at private colleges, $11,260 for state residents at public colleges, and $27,120 for out-of-state students at state schools, college is easily costing a staggering $200,000-plus when all is said and done.[30] That's a lot of money for college! And if you have more than one kid like me, now we are talking A LOT of money!

I know we parents feel pressure when it comes to saving for college. I will never forget working with a widow whose husband had suddenly died, only for her to discover he had secretly taken out a half million-dollar loan to pay for the children's colleges, which the estate had to pay off, leaving her with less money she thought she'd have to live on after his death. The husband did not want anyone, including his own family, to know he could not afford to pay for their education. I can only imagine the pressure he must have felt. I want to make sure all us parents have a good plan in place to fund this very important milestone.

There's also a lot of uncertainty for parents when it comes to saving for college. How do we know how much we should save when we don't know where our child will ultimately get admitted? How do we know if our child will even go to college? How do we know how much money we will be making at the time our child goes to college and whether they can qualify for any financial aid based on our household income?

While we can't anticipate everything, we can plan in a matter that leaves as many options on the table as possible and provides the funding for your ideal scenario when the time comes. Asking these three key questions will help shape your planning:

1. How much are we (the parents) willing to pay for college?

There are a variety of factors that will impact how much we as parents choose to pay for our children's college education (i.e. the value of a college education, the value of the college experience unrelated to academics, and our child's likelihood of making better connections and having better opportunities by going to a specific school). The one I will focus on here is how much we as parents can reasonably afford.

Most parents cannot afford to shell out $200,000 plus for college (especially per kid) without derailing their own financial security. With statistics showing that 89 percent of parents are in debt, 77 percent of us do not have a six-month emergency fund, and 50 percent of us are not saving for retirement, coming up with an extra $200,000 is no easy feat. That is why as early on as possible we must follow the Three Ps and develop an overall financial plan and see how saving for college fits into it.

Once you map out your overall financial goals, including for your own retirement (which we will address later in this chapter), then you can decide how much you can or are willing to pay for college and include a monthly contribution in your budget to save up. Obviously, the sooner you start, the longer the money can grow, and the interest can compound.

The biggest mistake I see my clients making is throwing money in their children's college savings accounts, thinking they'll get serious about saving for their own retirement after the kids have graduated, only to never catch up. I remember the frustration of a wife whose husband wanted them to sell their family home once it was time to retire because they still had a mortgage and were not financially prepared. Years earlier he had refinanced the home to pay for the kids' colleges and never caught back up. I don't want that to happen to you.

2. How much are we willing to allow our kids to go into debt paying for college?

College kids on average are graduating with $35,000 of student loan debt and will ultimately pay back much more because of interest.[31] Some families *need* their child to help pay for their schooling while others feel their child should help contribute as a matter of principle. If you want your child to contribute to the cost of college by taking out student loans, it is important to help them understand what taking on debt really means so they can make well informed choices.

Helping our kids understand how a student loan works—including how deferment works, how compounding interest works, how it's difficult to discharge student loans in bankruptcy, and how it can delay other important life milestones like graduate school, buying a home, marriage and kids, and other goals—should be discussed before school choices are made and before financial contracts are signed.

We also don't want to be send our kids the message of "go to the best school possible" without also discussing, with equal weight, "how we expect that to be paid for." Honest and candid conversations will not only prevent our children from feeling blindsided but can also help them make good choices when it comes to the cost of education.

I know of a family whose child was over the moon to get admitted to his dream school, only to be forced to leave after the first year because his parents declined to make the school's required contribution as part of the child's financial aid package. They also did not want their son going into massive debt—especially since another school, though less prestigious, was offering him a full ride if he would transfer. The son was crushed over his parents' decision. The emotional turmoil could have been prevented had the parents and their son discussed expectations before school commitments were made.

3. How can we make college more affordable?

The good news is that the sticker price for most universities is not what most students pay. That's because there are many financial programs to help lower the cost or other ways to get that degree from the university without going there all four years.

Maybe you send your kid to a junior college first for a fraction of the cost, one whose credits will transfer to the more expensive school for the remainder of your kid's degree. That way, they can still get the name, the connections, and the degree. Maybe there are financial aid programs or scholarships that can help bring down the cost. Maybe you can better strategize on how you save for college, so you are taking advantage of tax savings strategies. Find out early how you can possibly reduce the price tag of college to make it more affordable.

Did you know there are hundreds of thousands of scholarships based on academics, sports, race, gender, and strange things like the Zombie Apocalypse Scholarship ($2,000 for the student demonstrating the best plan to avoid zombies)? Seriously. It's important to research the different scholarships out there and see if your child is eligible.

There are also federal grants for students who come from families with a lower household income. These grants can help supplement the cost of education for kids whose families simply cannot afford it.

There are also low-interest student loans available for most college kids if they need to borrow money for their education (although that should be a last resort). And there are work-study programs that provide financial aid to students who work part-time at the university while they attend school.

Keep in mind that while the sticker price is often higher for private universities, sometimes their financial aid packages can make them competitive with the less expensive public-school options. It's also important to factor in the length of time your child will attend college, as some students can graduate faster at private schools where mandatory courses are more available than at higher populated schools, saving on an extra year of tuition, room, and board, which should be factored in when you compare.

Some universities even have endowments from alumni and will not let students graduate with debt. Understanding this should absolutely be factored in when choosing one school versus another.

Some private companies have college assistance programs where they help pay a portion of the tuition for employees.

Understanding all the different financial assistance out there can reduce the cost of college and save you and your kids money in the end!

How to Invest for College the Right Way

How many of us opened a 529 college savings plan when our kids were young and checked the "I'm saving for my kids' college" box? Most parents default to this formulaic investing approach to college savings rather than evaluating which college savings vehicles make the most sense given the family's unique financial circumstances and goals, or the amount of time left before their child will attend college.

There are many ways to save for our children's higher education, some of which you may already be doing—contributing to a 529 account, an UTMA account, a Roth IRA account, a money market savings account, and more. There are pros and cons for all these vehicles, but many of us parents choose one by default without an actual strategy or need.

We must evaluate which tactics make the most sense given our financial profile, our comfort level with investing in the market, the age of our kids when we begin saving for college, whether we need to reduce taxes, and our likely eligibility for financial aid, before we can decide which formula (or a combination of formulas) makes the most sense! Let's look at some options together now.

Popular College Savings Plans

529 PLANS

529 savings plans are very popular state-run college savings plans. Although the money you contribute must be post-tax dollars, your contributions in your 529 can grow tax-deferred, and you won't have to pay taxes when you pull it out as long as it's for tuition, room and board, books, supplies, or equipment. They also have high aggregate contribution limits, allowing you to fully fund the cost of college through the 529. Furthermore, 529s owned by a parent will typically have minimal impact on your child's eligibility for financial aid, although some schools may consider them when assessing their own financial awards for students.

But 529s may not be the best college savings vehicle for you, especially if you are in a lower tax bracket and are not concerned about reducing your tax liability. Furthermore, 529 accounts can only be used for educational expenses. What if your child does not go to college for whatever reason or did not need the full amount you saved? You must use it for another family member's education, or else you'll have to pay taxes and penalties.

It's also important to understand how the money in a 529 gets invested, as the options may be limited. You'll also want to make sure the investment strategies you are using within your 529 become more conservative the closer you get to withdrawing that money for college.

As a side note, there are prepaid tuition 529 plans that help you lock in the cost of today's tuition rates, although its significantly limited to certain schools and states.

UTMA

The Uniform Transfer to Minors Act (UTMA) accounts are an attractive way for us parents to gift our children money and have it invested as it grows, but still manage it on their behalf until they reach a certain age. It's a popular way to save for our children's college, but unlike a 529, the money does not have to be spent only on education.

The downside, of course, is that because the money can be used for other things, our child has a right to that money upon a certain age and may not choose to use it for their education as we intended. It can also count against them if they apply for financial aid and have negative tax consequences that traditional college saving accounts like a 529 avoid.

ROTH IRA

Most of us associate a Roth IRA as a savings vehicle for our own retirement, which I'll talk about extensively in the upcoming section on retirement. But what's great about a Roth IRA is that because contributions are made post tax, and then get invested, you can withdraw contributions (not earnings) to help pay for college tax-free after five years of making the contribution. And you won't have any penalty. There are annual caps on how much you can contribute, and this savings vehicle can be used in conjunction with other college saving vehicles. And because a Roth IRA is a retirement account, it's not typically counted against your child when they apply for financial aid.

An additional play that some families make is to have their child open up their own Roth IRA, using their own income, and use those contributions to save for college. This is popular for families who have their own business and pay their children for part-time work or for being featured in marketing or products for the family business, or if their children receive their own income from work.

Whole Life Insurance

Some parents save for college by purchasing a whole life insurance policy on their child. While this provides a death benefit, parents typically purchase these policies as a savings vehicle, as a portion of the monthly premiums can go toward a cash value account that can be used for any purpose, including college (when parents take out a loan against the cash value). The money in the cash value account gets invested and grows tax deferred and is not counted against the student for financial aid. While it's more flexible than the 529 because it can be used for any purpose, it has higher fees you'll want to fully understand.

SAVINGS ACCOUNT

Saving for college in a high yield savings account that earns a low interest rate can be a good idea, especially if your child is closer to college and you do not want to risk the money you've contributed getting lost in the market without adequate time to rebound before it's needed for tuition. But using this as your only strategy for saving for college, especially when the kids are young, leaves too many dollars on the table you could have likely earned had you included more aggressive investments as part of your overall strategy for growth.

How to Put Together a College Funding Plan

If you're now starting to rethink your college savings strategy (or lack of it), how it fits into your overall financial security, what student loan debt would mean for your child, how you can reduce the cost of college, and whether those top schools are worth it . . . well, then I consider this chapter mission accomplished. I strongly recommend you talk with a professional (who I will help you identify in the Players section) who focuses on helping families create a college funding plan.

While I want to help you reach your goal of funding your children's college, I don't want you to forget that if you are following the Three Ps and you still cannot afford to cut that huge check for college when the time comes, it does not mean you have invested any less in your child than other parents who can. Know that your example of integrity and financial responsibility, your time, your love, and your devotion to your kids is far more valuable in the end than any dollar amount you can possibly give them.

VACATIONS AND SPECIAL OCCASIONS

Life is meant to be enjoyed. As a busy parent myself, I sometimes forget that.

We've all heard the expression that we should stop and smell the roses. But as we get more and more focused on reaching our **If Life Were Perfect** goals, we should not forget to enjoy the journey. There should be a sweet spot between money flying out of our hands and holding it too tightly while racing toward the finish line. That's where budgeting for those fun things in life, like vacations and special occasions, comes in, along with enjoying those simple everyday moments.

My clients Ben* and Sumina* are in their late thirties and have already hit some big financial milestones. They do not have credit card debt, they paid off their cars, they paid off their student loans, and they are paying down the fifteen-year mortgage on their home. They left their desk jobs and are both self-employed, providing them the flexibility they longed for to spend more time with their growing kids. So why were they at odds when we sat down to discuss their finances? Sumina wanted to take a vacation and Ben thought it was a waste of money. She not only felt hurt but wanted to understand what the point of working so hard was if you couldn't enjoy any of it.

How many of us have argued with our spouse over how much to spend on a vacation or special occasion, or to have one at all? How many of us feel guilty inside when we splurge on vacations and special occasions, even when we are financially on track? There always seems to be an expense or investment for which money could be better spent. I think of my client who was strictly focused on building wealth and securing his family's future, only to have his wife pass away in her fifties before enjoying the vacations and special occasions they intended to enjoy *one day*.

While some of us feel that vacations are a waste of money, research shows that they are imperative to our overall health and success. Taking a break can lower your stress, lessen the risk of heart disease and other health problems, boost your mental health by providing you a better outlook on life, and improve your relationships. Surprisingly, taking a vacation results in your feeling *more* motivation to achieve your **If Life Were Perfect** goals![32] It's no different than refueling your car, or recharging your body by getting a good night's sleep. You can accomplish far more when you stop to enjoy these well needed breaks.

Planning and enjoying a special occasion can also bring health benefits. It can foster a sense of gratitude as we celebrate the special people we love. From birthdays, to holidays, to graduations, to anniversary and weddings, all these occasions can remind us how blessed we really are. We deserve to celebrate ourselves, too.

We parents should have something to look forward to, especially when our days are long. Research shows that planning a trip can bring you more joy than the actual trip itself.[33] How many of us enjoyed planning our own wedding as much as the day itself? (Just nod your head yes!)

The wealthy understand this secret when it comes to enjoying life. Statistics show they spend their money on experiences over things, as they understand the lasting value that travel and special occasions can bring.

Spending money on vacations and special occasions really is a necessity for reaching our **If Life Were Perfect** goals and enjoying our journey along the way. But we must plan for these vacations and special occasions wisely so we can enjoy them without freaking out over the cost. We all remember the film *Father of the Bride* with Steve Martin when his character tore the hot dog buns apart at the store because he was stressed out about paying for his daughter's wedding and thought he was being overcharged! We don't want to melt down when we are supposed to be celebrating.

First: Your vacation or special occasion must be realistic

Who would not love a lavish trip to Italy or one day hosting their child's ideal wedding celebration? And while following the Three Ps in this book can help you get there, we must be realistic about what we can afford.

A realistic trip or event is one that fits within your current budget and overall financial goals. For those of us who are still deep in credit card debt, a quick staycation or an at-home birthday party makes a lot more sense than something lavish. But for those of us who have hit more financial milestones and have more cash to spare, there's nothing wrong—in fact, there's a lot right!—with splurging on a big trip or special celebration now and then.

I know as parents we can feel pressure to do bigger things. We see other parents posting photos of their kids in Hawaii while we take our kids to Target. But there was no research I could find supporting the idea that a trip or event must be extravagant to provide the benefits that come from these experiences. Think back to your vacations and special events before you had kids and when you were a kid, and I bet they were all special in their own way regardless of the cost. The key is to plan a trip or special occasion that can be enjoyed worry-free of the expense.

Second: You must identify the timing for these milestones

When to celebrate special occasions is usually not a mystery. They tend to be on our radar. But many of us are unsure how often we should be taking vacations, especially those bigger trips. How big and how often will likely come down to your schedule, your obligations, and your money. Research shows that you must take at least one vacation per year to reduce a variety of health risks.[34] Many parents also use their paid vacation days from work as a guide for what's appropriate. You can also consider shorter trips and spread them out throughout the year and still enjoy those secondary benefits.

Like everything else, a vacation or celebration cannot happen unless it is on your calendar. So, take a moment and pull yours out and block out those dates. For Josh and I, we typically took our bigger trips or did something to celebrate when we completed a financial milestone as a high-five to ourselves before tackling the next one. Everyone can identify where to best fit these trips in to enjoy life and motivate ourselves to keep going on our financial journeys.

Third: You must budget for vacations and special occasions

We all know that an all-expense paid trip would be amazing, or having someone else footing the bill for a party would be fantastic, but typically we as parents will have to fund our own vacations and special occasions. This can cause fights among spouses or internal guilt over how much one should spend.

I am going to help you (and your spouse) stop wrestling over these expenses right now. That's because now that you've decided what's realistic and how much a trip or celebration should cost given your current financial circumstances, you must add in a line item expense in your budget that is specifically earmarked for vacations and special occasions. Then, each month, you can save that money toward the trip or event you have in mind. Once it is in your budget, then it is paid for in advance and you can really enjoy it.

I hope you are one huge step closer to taking that well deserved trip! I hope you are one step closer to celebrating something special! And for all you spouses out there married to someone too tight with money—you're welcome!

REDEFINING RETIREMENT

Retirement is a huge life milestone we spend many years trying to reach. But let's be honest with each other and really think about what comes to mind when we hear the word "retirement." Maybe you think of something that seems forever far away. Maybe you think of your parents and what they are doing in their retirements. Maybe you think of your 401(k) account that some of your paycheck goes toward each month. Or maybe you picture someone older blowing out a candle on a retirement cake before talking about the cruises they plan to take.

I work with a lot of retired people and can tell you their lives vary drastically depending on the choices they made back when they were our age. Some of them are having the time of their lives with their shiny silver hair and designer golf clothes, living in their recently remodeled family home and treating the entire family to vacations.

But other seniors I help are on the complete opposite end of the spectrum and are struggling to get by. They are living in a tiny apartment or at a family member's home and need financial help from their adult children or the government.

And then there is everyone in between, with some more prepared for retirement than others. Statistics show that two out of three seniors cannot retire because they need the money from working income, and that many seniors are living so long now because of modern medicine that they are outliving their money. The average life expectancy they were financially preparing for has increased well beyond those predictions.

Regardless of financial status, many seniors get hit with massive health care costs above what the government will cover. As seniors continue to age, especially during their final years, many of them need assistance with their daily living activities. Wealthy seniors can afford caregivers, extra medical treatments, and to live in their own family home. Middle class seniors with major health problems often end up losing their family home paying for their health care costs and leaving the healthy spouse broke. And seniors with little money can get help from the government for their caregiving needs, but it is not the level of care you would want for someone you love.

The reason I am telling you all this is because you need to think about what group you are *planning* to be in when you retire. Not *hoping* to be in, but *planning* to be in. How do you want your story to end? Statistics show that 50 percent of us parents are not saving at all for retirement, and most of the rest of us are not saving nearly enough. Are you confident you are making the sacrifices necessary today to secure your future?

I hope I've shocked you a little bit because I don't like seeing so many seniors struggling to get by, and I certainly do not want you to be one of them. I hope you are not looking at your 401(k) account or other retirement plans as something that's cutting into your paycheck, but rather as something that's securing your future. Those retirement accounts will be the lifesavers you need in your later years, ensuring you can age with dignity and enjoy the quality of life you want.

It is time to break free of the statistics and redefine our retirement as our golden years and not our penny-pinching years. Here are the main things you need to know to start securing your future:

Time Matters

I told you earlier how if you began investing $200 per month beginning at age thirty-five with a 7 percent return that you'll earn more than *double* what you would have by age sixty-five than if you had waited to begin those contributions until age forty-five. That's primarily because of how compounding interest works: each time you make interest on your investment, that interest gets incorporated back into the principal causing it to grow, and then interest gets applied again and again. Many of us did not save enough when we were younger and need to make up for lost time. We're late to the game, and now we must save even more every month.

Now, don't let "lost time" deter you from getting serious about saving for retirement now. If you switch to an investment mentality and start contributing now, you will see those dollars go up each month and increase as they get properly invested. Even starting this year as opposed to next year will make a significant difference in terms of your growth and what you will ultimately have.

Understand How Much You Must Save

How much you need to set aside each month toward retirement depends on how old you are today, how much you have already saved for retirement, what age you wish to have the option to retire by, what lifestyle you wish to have in retirement, what your potential medical costs may be, and how long you are statistically expected to live. Those are a lot of factors that need to be considered when calculating the numbers!

There are also rules and restrictions for retirement accounts that affect how much you can contribute to them annually, which impacts how quickly you can build up your principal, as we will talk more about in a minute.

There's a big misconception that we must save money for our retirement so there's enough in our accounts to draw down from each month to pay for our lifestyle and needs until we either die or have depleted all our money. But that's not how it works best!

Financial experts agree that ideally you will save up enough money by the time you retire so you can live off the income your money generates each month from your principle through conservative investments, and not draw down the principal at all![35] The more you withdraw the principal, the less money you have to continue to conservatively invest, and the less income you can generate to live on. That's what we mean when we say you want to live off your family nest egg!

So how do you know the exact amount you need for your family nest egg and how much you should be saving for retirement every month and year? Beyond determining what your ideal lifestyle will cost, potential medical bills, and how long you will likely live, you must also factor in having extra cash for unforeseen emergencies, any withdrawals required by law, and the cost of inflation (when the cost of living goes up each year, making your dollar less valuable). There are plenty of online calculators and financial advisors who can help you determine the actual number using these factors. Then you will know how much you must save and invest to get there.

Retirement Accounts Are Special!

Now let's talk about saving and investing for our retirement, as there are unique saving vehicles specifically designed for life after full-time work. Retirement accounts are unlike non-retirement accounts in specific ways. While the money in your retirement accounts also gets invested, retirement accounts have rules and protections in place so that the money will be there when you need it most.

Most retirement accounts allow you to contribute to them using "pre-tax" money, which gets invested and grows tax free until you make withdrawals. How much you can contribute is limited by law, too. Plus, the government has something called "mandatory distributions" once you reach age seventy-two, and you will have to pay taxes on those withdrawals.

Retirement accounts are also unique in that many employers have matching programs where they will contribute a percentage of your annual contributions, which the employer can then deduct on their federal corporate income tax return. If you are an employee, you should find out how much your employer will match. Some employers actually match dollar for dollar! That's a 100 percent return on your investment into your retirement account! Here's what is shocking, though. Many of us don't take full advantage of the matching programs from employers, which can result in significantly less money in your retirement account![36] (As we talked about earlier, this is why most financial experts will tell you to contribute to your company's retirement plan if your employer matches your contribution, even if you have credit card debt!)

What about pre-retirement withdrawals? Usually, you can't withdraw the money in your retirement account before you hit a certain age without having to pay penalties and taxes (except for the Roth IRA, which I'll tell you about). Different retirement accounts have different rules, but the idea is that your money will be there for you in your retirement years.

And finally, retirement accounts are special because they often have asset protection, meaning if someone sues you, they can go after your home or other investments, but cannot take the money inside your retirement accounts.

THE FAMILY NEST EGG

Popular Retirement Accounts

Each retirement account comes with its own unique set of rules and regulations. Which kind of account you choose will come down to your age, how much money you make each year, whether you are an employee or self-employed, and what your company offers.

Let's look together at your best options through your employer, or through self-funding, and see what makes sense for you. It's possible that you may use a hybrid approach where you are contributing to both your employer sponsored retirement plan and an individual retirement plan, both being subject to contribution limits and tax deduction limitations.

EMPLOYER SPONSORED RETIREMENT PLANS

Many companies offer retirement plans to help you save for your retirement. Let's take a look at the most popular employer sponsored retirement plans so you will have a great frame of reference when checking to see what's available where you work.

401(K), 403(B), AND 457

The names for these retirement accounts reference the sections in the Internal Revenue Code that govern them. Each section lays out a way an employer can create a retirement plan for employees to contribute pre-tax dollars into investments. Currently, as a plan participant, you can contribute up to $19,500 a year, plus an extra $6,500 if you have hit the big five-oh! And, you can decide if you want your contributions to get invested more conservatively or aggressively. Many employers have employee matching programs that I mentioned earlier.

If you withdraw money from these retirement accounts before you reach retirement age (currently set by law at fifty-nine and a half), you'll typically get hit with a 10 percent early withdrawal penalty and have to pay taxes on what you withdraw. While it is true that some retirement plans allow you to take out a loan against your 401(k) (borrowing from yourself basically), that can result, among other negative consequences, in less money in the end. Why? The funds you borrowed won't be earning investment returns like they would have had they stayed invested. There are also payback requirements that may be difficult to meet if life circumstances change. You'd want to really understand the consequences for an early withdrawal or loan before executing either one.

SIMPLE IRA

Short for "Individual Retirement Account," this plan is for employees of smaller businesses and has similar rules and regulations to a 401(k), but the contribution limits are lower. Currently you can contribute $12,500 a year, and an additional $3,000 if you are over fifty. Employers may match up to a certain percentage.

SOLO 401(K) AND SEP IRA

These retirement accounts are for those who are self-employed or are small business owners. The Solo 401(k) and the SEP IRA (Simplified Employee Pension) have similar rules and regulations to a 401(k), but the SEP IRA allows the employer to contribute up to 25 percent of their income, or $55,000, whichever is less, and you cannot make catch-up contributions. So, if you have a side hustle, do not overlook this great option! You also have more options on how your investments are made, options that are less likely when you are a participant in a larger company plan.

PENSION FUNDS

Unlike the other employer sponsored retirement plans, a pension plan is created and *funded* by your employer and will provide you a monthly income in your retirement years. What you ultimately get is determined by your salary, age of retirement, and the number of years you have worked at your company. The pension plan may even come with a death benefit for your loved ones.

Now that you understand what plans may be available through your work, let's take a look at your options for setting up your own retirement plan.

Individual Retirement Accounts

Not all of us work for a company that offers a retirement plan. Or, even if we do, our employer may not match contributions, so there's less incentive to use that plan over an individual one we can better control.

IRA

Anyone can open their own IRA and contribute $6,000 a year, or $7,000 if you're fifty or older. An IRA is funded by your pre-tax dollars, and then the money grows tax free until you must begin taking your mandatory distributions, at which time you'll pay income tax. However, if you are heavily contributing to your company plan, this may impact your ability to defer taxes in your IRA. You'll want to talk with your tax professional.

ROTH IRA

While a Roth IRA is also an individual retirement account, it has very specific rules that others don't. It was created as part of the Tax Relief Act of 1997 and named after the chief legislative sponsor, Senator William Roth. The main difference between the Roth IRA and other retirement accounts is that you first pay taxes on any of your contributions to a Roth IRA, but then it can grow tax free and be withdrawn tax free once you are age fifty-nine and a half. So, if you are planning on being in a higher tax bracket when you are retiring than you are now, then the Roth IRA makes a lot of sense! Plus, unlike other retirement accounts, you can withdraw your contributions to your Roth IRA (not earnings) after five years of making them without a penalty. That's huge! You're also not required to take minimum distributions, since the government would not get paid on them anyway.

The downside of the Roth IRA, and why not everyone has one, is that they are only available for those of us making under $135,000 as a single person or $199,000 for us married couples combined.

There is also a Roth IRA conversion that allows you to transfer retirement funds from a traditional IRA or 401(k) into a Roth account, but you will need to pay the income taxes you had deferred on the other retirement accounts. The Roth IRA conversion is also an option for high income earners who have a random low-income tax year (i.e. business was slow).

BRINGING IT ALL TOGETHER

As we conclude this retirement section, let me break it down to one simple sentence: You must start saving for retirement right now! I know it's easy to glaze over these different retirement strategies and just see numbers and letters and labels, but I want you to read through these saving vehicles again and see them for the dream makers they are and for the future miracles you will need. Whether you choose one retirement vehicle over another or opt for a hybrid approach, what matters most is that you have a strategy, you select the best plan(s), and you are on track to enjoy your golden years and age with dignity.

And as we conclude the Funding Life Milestones chapter, I hope you have a better understanding now of how to best prepare for these landmark moments, and that you enjoy the journey along the way. You can enjoy today while securing tomorrow, I am sure, and I wish you many happy memories to come.

6

PLAYING THE TAX GAME

REMEMBER THE BUDGET SECTION WHERE we discussed how to reduce our expenses and use those extra dollars to get what we really want most—like those things on our **If Life Were Perfect** list? Well, guess what substantial expense, probably the biggest, might be? You may have overlooked it.

Taxes!

Taxes are, by far, most families' biggest expense. If you do not believe me, just look at your gross wage amount versus what you deposit in your bank account and you can see what I am talking about. Look at what the sales tax was for each of your purchases just for yesterday alone. Look at your semi-annual property tax bill for your home. You are paying up the wazoo in taxes and it is costing you your financial security!

Now, don't worry. I would never advocate for us not to pay our taxes, because let's face it, someone has to pay for the roads and schools, and no one looks good in a prison jump suit. But what I want to advocate for is paying your *fair share* of taxes, not a dollar less and not a dollar more! The problem is that too many of us are over-paying our taxes because we do not understand how to properly determine our fair share.

We all know that the government has rules on what taxes we must pay, but what too many of us do not know are all the exceptions the government has written into its tax code. It's like when you tell your teenager their curfew is midnight, but make an exception for when he is spending the night at a friend's, or there's a big school dance or party, or the football game is far away, or a movie is almost finished, etc. The key to taxes is understanding both the *rule* and the *exceptions*, and *then* paying your fair share. Most of us just hear the rule and then write the big fat check!

Imagine how many dollars you could keep on the table if you (and your tax professional) understood both the government's tax rules and exceptions, and then paid your fair share. Imagine if you strategically began making your financial decisions to maximize your tax savings. Here are five things you absolutely must understand about taxes so you never overpay your fair share again:

1. The government uses taxes to incentivize you to behave a certain way.

The government wants to reward you for making certain choices and will let you pay less in taxes if you do as they wish.

Have you ever wondered why you get a tax break for driving an electric car but not for buying a gas guzzling SUV? It's because the government wants to incentivize and reward you for buying a product that helps support the government's goal of cleaner air.

Or maybe you wonder why the government gives you a tax break each year for being a parent. It's because the government likes that you are paying for your own kids so they don't have to, and that you are birthing future taxpayers.

Or maybe you know that the government taxes the sale of cigarettes much more than fruit. Well, the government wants to deter you from smoking because it's bad for your health and healthy citizens reduce the burden on the health care system.

While those are some common examples of how the government incentivizes you through taxes to behave a certain way, the government extends these incentives to all aspects of your personal finances. If you understand and choose the behaviors that the government wants you to engage in, then they will reward you with lower taxes. It's just like when you give your kid a reward for doing extra chores but ground them when they blow them off. Understand what those behaviors are and save yourself a fortune.

2. Employees pay the most taxes.

If you work for another person and receive a paycheck, you will likely pay a much higher percentage of your income and earnings to taxes than your boss does on his or hers. Why? The government believes that your boss is helping carry out the government's big goal of creating jobs, and they will reward your business-owner boss through tax breaks for engaging in behaviors the government encourages.

Therefore, employers get all sorts of tax breaks you do not get as an employee. They can write off "business expenses" such as vehicle purchases, their home office, meals and entertainment, payroll, marketing and advertising, all of which lower the amount they must pay tax on. They can even employ the tax strategy known as income shifting, where they shift their personal income to their minor children (who are in the lower tax brackets) by paying their children for appearing on the company website or ads, or for helping around the office. This results in the parents having less taxable income at their higher tax bracket. Remember, these aren't "loopholes," but are deemed legitimate, government-sanctioned tax reduction strategies!

3. Certain investments get more favorable tax treatment than others.

So, it's clear that choosing to start a business offers far more tax incentives and savings than choosing to work for someone else. But if being a business owner isn't in the cards, there are lots of investments that come with tax incentives or savings because the government wants you to choose them.

For example, the government wants you to save for your child to go to college, so they have incentivized you to contribute to their 529 college savings plan. Although your contributions are not tax deductible, the earnings you accrue through the investments within a 529 plan grow tax-free and you will not pay taxes when you withdraw the money for college.

The same goes for your retirement savings plans. The government wants you to save for your retirement, so they will let you contribute pre-tax dollars to your 401(k), and let it grow tax deferred until you withdraw it when you retire. Or, they will let you contribute post-tax dollars to a Roth IRA but let it grow tax free and be withdrawn tax free for your retirement. But if, on the other hand, you open up a regular savings account and contribute to that for use in your retirement years, you won't get any tax incentives. Can you see how the government motivated you to save for retirement the way it thinks is best? They incentivized you to save for your retirement in a more restricted account, making it more likely the money will be there for your retirement, and therefore less likely the government will have to fully support you.

For your other investments in taxable accounts, the government will incentivize you to invest in companies within the US that provide qualified dividends and/or provide long term capital gains. Both of these forms of income have preferential tax rates which are much lower than regular marginal income tax rates. The purpose of this preferential tax rate is to encourage investing within the border of our own country, and to invest in US assets for a long duration of time. (Long term capital gains must be held for a year and a day.)

The government also wants you to own a home. They don't reward you for renting, but they'll allow you to deduct your mortgage interest and real estate taxes on your home, so you are paying less in taxes. Or they will incentivize you to invest in real estate rental property by allowing you to depreciate the cost of the building each year, which lowers your tax liability. Again, they are motivating you to buy property through tax incentives that result in lower taxes for you.

The government also wants you to be charitable and take care of others who need your help. Whether it's a small donation or setting up a charitable foundation, there are tax rewards and incentives for those who share their wealth.

I could continue, but the point is that before you make any financial decision, you must understand how taxes are a factor! Choosing investments that the government encourages often results in massive tax savings.

4. Tax credits are free money.

Unlike tax deductions (which only reduce how much of your income will be taxed), tax credits, on the other hand, reduce the amount of tax you owe by providing you a dollar for dollar deduction. The government will give you tax credits for everything from the number of kids you have, to pursuing an education, to contributing to your retirement. It's important to understand whether you are eligible for these tax credits; sometimes, if you make too much money, these credits are not extended to you.

5. Tax planning and tax returns are not the same thing!

How many of us wait until early April each year to fill out a tax return form, cross our fingers, and hope we'll get a refund? Or maybe we buy a do-it-yourself program and trust that we can somehow, long after having made every financial decision that year, capture what's deductible and thereby lower our taxes? I'm shaking my head right now and begging you to please switch to a tax planning mentality to save yourself from overpaying your taxes!

Tax planning is when you look at every single financial decision *before* you make it, and then choosing to engage in behaviors that will result in lowering your taxes. It's understanding the tax implications *before* you sell your home and get hit with capital gains taxes that you never knew were a thing. It's selecting one retirement vehicle over another because you understand how that affects your taxes today *and* later when you retire. It's even choosing whether to stay at your current job or taking a leap and starting a business because of the massive amount of taxes you will save when you are a business owner. Do you know how many calls I get the last week of December, because my business owner and investor clients are doing all sorts of deals to reduce their tax liability before the year comes to an end?

At the end of the day, we all must earn a living, pay for expenses, invest, and save for the future. Understanding how the government will tax each and every choice you make can save you a lot of financial resources in the end. Please pay your fair share of taxes— not a dollar less or a dollar more!

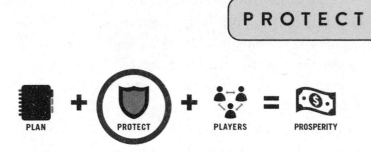

PLAN + PROTECT + PLAYERS = PROSPERITY

When I began my career as a lawyer, I had to do a short rotation in the law firm's bankruptcy department. I went in under the impression that people who filed for bankruptcy had gone on crazy buying sprees or made terrible business deals.

I remember very clearly one of the first cases that came across my desk. A woman had gone through cancer and was now filing for bankruptcy. As I looked through her debts and delved into her backstory, I found out that she was a parent stunned by her diagnosis, bombarded with massive health care bills because her health insurance would only cover so much, jobless because she had been on leave too long getting medical treatments, and reliant on credit cards to survive and feed her family.

If you think her story is shocking, it is. If you think her story is uncommon, sadly, it is not.

Regular, everyday parents just like you and me have terrible storms come into their lives—an illness or accident, a job loss or business failing, a lawsuit, a divorce, or the death of a loved one. These crises completely wipe them out financially and destroy all they've worked for. We all witnessed too many families around us become victims of the economic devastation of COVID-19. I sincerely hope that your family was not one of them.

Storms in life will come. We can't change the weather. And no one wants to end up on the GoFundMe page or with the for-sale sign outside their family home because they were not prepared.

Let's take a lesson from mother nature. You may have heard that bison will charge straight through the eye of a storm and survive, while cows, their domesticated relatives, will turn and try to outrun a storm. The cow ends up running *with* a storm and suffering badly. My question for you is, how do you want to face those storms in life—like the bison, or like the cow?

The next few chapters of this book will help you prepare for the "what-if" scenarios in life that I sincerely hope will skip your families. Do not be afraid to contemplate these possibilities. Instead, commit right now to planning the most effective way to weather them. As an estate planning lawyer who works everyday with families dealing with crisis, I will walk you through the financial, legal, and practical steps you must take to protect yourself, your assets, and your loved ones, no matter what life may bring.

You are the bison.

7

THE FAMILY
EMERGENCY FUND

WHERE WERE YOU WHEN YOU heard your city was shutting down due to COVID-19 and that you were to grab your essential supplies from work and go get the kids from school? Did you think the shutdown would last for a week? Did you think it would mean you'd lose your job or your business? Did you do the math within the first day at home to try to figure out how long your family could survive if another paycheck never came? How financially prepared did you feel to weather such an unexpected storm?

As a family trust attorney, I have a front-row seat to people's life emergencies when they reach out to me in their time of need. I receive the calls when clients have lost their job or business, received a diagnosis, been handed divorce papers, or even lost a spouse or child. These families wake up one day believing all is well, only to have life change so quickly.

On top of the emotional nightmare, there's the financial fallout many families experience when disaster strikes. We all witnessed how COVID-19 hit people we knew with job loss within the first week of the stay-at-home orders as businesses were forced to close. As it continued for months upon months, many of us watched our family and friends financially suffer. I sincerely hope this did not happen to you.

There's a 100 percent chance that we will experience a major life emergency at some point, and yet the majority of us parents are not financially prepared for one. In fact, 77 percent of us families *do not* have at least six months' worth of living expenses saved in an emergency fund for a crisis.[37]

It's challenging. I understand. There are so many other competing financial needs that saving for an emergency fund can get overlooked. We reassure ourselves that we could figure it out when the disaster occurs, or in a worst case scenario live off a credit card, tap into our 401(k), pull some equity out of our home, get government assistance, or whatever we think will help get our family through.

And yes, you could do those things. You could turn to credit cards and rack up debt, and later try to dig yourself out of from that hole on top of paying all the new expenses that will come.

Yes, you could tap into your 401(k) or retirement account and later try to pay back all the money you borrowed, plus the penalties, taxes, and fees, and lost interest, and hope to still retire on time.

Yes, you could take out equity from your home and gamble with the roof over your head, pay new fees and closing costs, hope the interest rates will be low, and reset the clock on your loan.

And yes, you could rely on the government, hoping that unemployment payments or food stamps will be enough to support the basic needs of your family.

Or you can set money aside now before the crisis hits. You can create a family emergency fund!

DEFINING A TRUE EMERGENCY

A true emergency is a public or personal crisis that you could not have reasonably anticipated, one that negatively impacts *your* finances above and beyond what proper insurance can mitigate.

A friend once told me a funny story about her college-aged daughter. When she sent her daughter off to school, she gave her a credit card that was only to be used in an absolute emergency.

That is, if she could not first contact her mom for help or use other money. One day, the daughter called her mom to let her know she had to use the credit card for an emergency. Obviously concerned, my friend asked what happened, and her daughter said very seriously, "Well, Mom, Taylor Swift tickets went on sale last night and I was in the waiting room and had to buy them right then or lose my chance." While apparently the show was great, that was not what her mom had in mind as an emergency.

We can laugh at this, but we adults can also confuse what really is and is not a true emergency. We rely on our emergency funds for extra expenses we should have anticipated, like the dishwasher going out or a kid needing a cavity filled. We know day-to-day extra expenses arise and that we should have extra cash for them. But getting laid off, on the other hand, because your business was shut down during the pandemic is not something any of us reasonably foresaw coming. Now, that's a true emergency.

There are expenses we should see coming. Let's not be the ones to find that our emergency fund money is no longer there when we actually need it to survive.

WHAT DOES AN EMERGENCY FUND LOOK LIKE?

A family emergency fund is a cash reserve of six to nine months of basic living expenses for an unanticipated public or personal crisis. Its sole purpose is for, let's say it together, *emergencies*, and it is locked away from all other financial accounts. It can be accessed without triggering any penalties, fees, or taxes. For this reason, keeping your family emergency fund in a high interest savings account is ideal because it is easy to access and can bring in a small return as it grows from the compounding interest.

Some financial experts only recommend three months of living expenses, but with the devastating and long term effects we saw from COVID-19, we should anticipate that another public crisis or disaster could last far longer than three months. I've also seen many of my clients battle cancer or long-term illnesses, where a three month's savings is simply not enough.

You might be thinking right now, *I don't have that much money to set aside for an emergency*. Six to nine months is a long time. Yes, it is a long time, but keep in mind it is only six to nine months of *basic* living expenses, meaning the bare minimum amount of money you'll need to cover food, shelter, water, electricity, gas, health insurance costs, minimum payments on bills, and any other bare necessities your family needs to survive.

I know a husband who had a great paying job while his wife looked after their four children at home. One afternoon, he had to go into his boss's office to get something off his desk. He saw a note there. His boss was writing a list of employees he intended to lay off because of financial trouble. Guess whose name was on that list? Knowing his job firing was imminent, the husband and wife immediately cut out every single expense they had other than the family's most basic needs. This included going out to dinner and all the children's activities, like dance lessons and karate. They even temporarily stopped contributing to their children's college savings accounts so they could save every dollar possible in an emergency fund to provide for the family's basic needs until he could find a new job. Ironically, a few months later, the owner called the husband in, told him he had let the boss go, and that he was being promoted.

Now, I wish all our family emergencies could have that happy ending, but we know that's not always the case. There's nothing worse than feeling like you could be out on the street or not have food for your own kid. That's why you need a family emergency fund.

Is it Better to Use Money for an Emergency Reserve or to Pay Off Bills?

Saving for a family emergency fund is the very first financial milestone a family should hit after they pay off their credit cards in full.

We talked earlier about the pitfalls of credit card debt and how that compounding interest drags you down in a hole and buries you with little way out. For this reason, there is not a compelling reason to stock-pile cash when you are already in the hole. It makes far more sense to keep some cash on hand, but first dig your way out of the hole, and then begin saving for your family emergency fund.

While I understand you may also have a car payment or mortgage that is accumulating interest, you at least have an asset attached to your car payment or mortgage that you could sell if you must, while a credit card debt is for personal items with less value or things you've already used or consumed. In other words, your credit cards are not secured by an asset you can sell if you cannot make the payments.

Now is the Time to Save

I will take this point even further than most financial experts. If you do not have an emergency reserve at this moment, that is a true emergency in and of itself. Go back to your budget, go to your bare bone expenses, and immediately save up (after those credit cards are paid off, of course).

You do not know what tomorrow will bring. You do not know whether your business will take off or if your company will succeed. You don't know if you will wake up tomorrow with a strange lump. You don't know when you or your spouse will leave this earth. You can plan for the best in life, and you can hope for the best in life, but you cannot simply sit back and count on the best in life. That is why it is imperative to prepare for the "what-ifs" today, so you can endure them tomorrow.

Throwing you into crisis mode before one happens may feel extreme. Most financial experts will tell you to save up money from your annual tax return or a random bonus to slowly build up a reserve. But I will tell you that as an estate planning attorney who sits with families in their darkest of hours, it is night and day between those who were prepared and those who were not. Even one month of a reserve is better than none.

Tell yourself, in fact promise yourself, that you will start right now. With each month worth of basic living expenses that you save, buy a LifeSavers candy and place it next to a photo of your kids until you get to six. That emergency fund will indeed be your lifesaver.

8

INSURANCE & ASSET PROTECTION

THERE ARE CERTAIN MAJOR LIFE emergencies that even an adequate family emergency fund cannot fully mitigate. The silver lining, though, is that there are typically insurance or asset protection options to protect you from absorbing the brunt of the cost. You can think of this chapter as the seatbelt chapter, so you can protect yourself in case you get hit.

LIFE INSURANCE

Jay* and his wife were in their early forties when they came to me for help setting up a family trust for themselves and their two young children. I noticed that Jay, who was the sole financial provider for the family, did not have any life insurance. When I told him he needed it, he was adamantly opposed. He thought it was a waste of money considering his low odds of prematurely dying. I found it surprising that Jay was willing to spend money on a trust but not on a life insurance policy. Suddenly and tragically, Jay died before getting a life insurance policy in place. His wife was left to support the kids, which was challenging given that she'd been out of the workforce for some time caring for the children. Eventually, she had to sell the family home and move out of state to get her education and start over. It was simply devastating and completely avoidable had Jay had proper life insurance.

Too many of us are playing the odds like Jay. We're leaving our families at great risk of financial insecurity by not having life insurance. Life insurance is a contract you can secure between yourself and an insurance company where, in exchange for you paying a monthly premium, they will give your family money if you pass away.

There are two main types of life insurance: term life insurance (Term) and whole life insurance (Whole). As a side note, universal and variable life insurance work similarly to Whole. Term will provide you a death benefit if you die within a predetermined number of years from when you secured the policy, but if you die after the policy expires, your beneficiary will not get the death benefit and you cannot recoup any of the premiums you had paid. Whole covers you for life with a death benefit and has a cash value component where a portion of your premiums gets placed in a savings account for your benefit.

While Whole sounds great on the surface, it is typically way more expensive than Term, and many financial experts believe that we Gen X and Millennial parents are better off going with the less expensive Term and investing the extra money we would have spent on Whole.

Rather than go deep sea diving into the mechanics of these different policies (there's no shortage of information on that), I want to focus our discussion on the top five mistakes I see most families make when it comes to life insurance. This will save you and your family a great deal of confusion and devastation if anything happens to you.

Mistake #1: Not understanding what type of policy you have

Many people do not understand what type of life insurance policy they have, forgetting whether they chose Term or Whole (or a variation of Whole). It's critical to know which kind you are paying for, as it affects your overall financial plan for your family. If you think you have Whole and that the insurance company is saving a portion of your monthly premium in a savings account, but you later realize that you had Term, then you are obviously not saving for the future the way you thought. Or if you are expecting a death benefit to be there no matter when you die, but you only have Term that may first expire, then you may not be leaving behind enough money for your surviving spouse to live on.

You must contact your financial advisor or your insurance policy carrier to find out what type of insurance you have and how that affects your overall financial plan while you are living, and after you pass.

Mistake #2: Not knowing how much coverage you have

Families fill out a disclosure form when I meet with them, noting how much life insurance they have and who issued the policies. Most people do not know the amount of coverage they have. Is it $100,000, $500,000, a million, or more? Often, they secured life insurance through their employer and are unsure of the final payout.

They also don't understand whether their policy will cover *any* type of death, or only an accidental death. You can imagine how shocking it is when someone passes away from cancer, only to find that their loved-one's employee-issued life insurance policy only covered accidents like a car wreck. You need to contact your employer and find out which causes of death are covered and which are not. If you secured your own policy outside of work, I suggest you contact your financial advisor or the company you bought the policy from.

Mistake #3: Not having the right amount of life insurance

Most families do not have the right amount of life insurance coverage, often because they don't fully understand the purpose of life insurance and what it should cover. Yes, they know life insurance is there to help provide for their dependents (i.e. spouse and kids), but they don't consider all the costs it should cover.

I often hear people say, "We have enough insurance to pay off the mortgage, with some left over until my spouse can go back to work." This approach leaves families at financial risk. There won't be enough life insurance money for the surviving spouse to reach all their financial goals and have enough money to live on through their retirement years.

As a general rule of thumb, most financial experts agree that life insurance should cover twenty times your beneficiaries' income needs if you pass away. Remember, once your spouse is past their working years, they will ideally have enough money in a family nest egg to live off the *interest*, rather than draining the principal. Keep in mind that even if your spouse has a high paying job, their bills won't get cut in half when you pass away, and in fact will likely increase over time because of inflation. Why put them in a financial crunch when it can easily be avoided through proper life insurance coverage? Be sure to secure the right amount so your loved one can have complete financial security if you're no longer here.

Mistake #4: Not having insurance for the stay-at-home spouse

We know how much goes into running a household and looking after the kids. From laundry to dishes and carpools to playdates, everyday tasks really add up. Some families pay for outside help with these activities, while others do not. We all know how expensive childcare and household help can be!

Too many families fail to factor in the cost of running a household and childcare when they evaluate their life insurance needs. If you have a spouse who stays at home and handles all this while you are away at your job, think about how life would drastically change for you were they not there. For this reason, make sure you have life insurance on the stay-at-home spouse so that you—as the work-outside-the-home spouse—could have the financial flexibility you need to either hire outside help for those activities or cut back at work to handle them yourself.

And on that note, can we all take a second here to give a nod to our single parents here, who singlehandedly manage all the finances, childcare, and household duties? We see you and know it is not easy. I hope we are all reaching out and supporting you however we can.

Mistake #5: Naming the wrong beneficiary

Please, whatever you do, make sure your beneficiary on your life insurance policy is the person you want to benefit!

We had a client come to us for help because her husband had passed away, and his life insurance policy had his mother listed as the beneficiary—not his wife! Unfortunately, the husband had not updated his life insurance beneficiary form when he got married. Now, you would think that the husband's mom would have given the money to the wife considering that she was left to raise three young children on her own. But she did not. She took the position that her late son must have wanted *her* to have the money over his own wife and young children, simply because he did not update the form. If you think this would never happen, then believe me, money and grief can have strange effects on people!

Life insurance companies will pay out the money from your policy to whomever you listed as the beneficiary on the policy. That means if you still have your parents or an ex-spouse listed as your beneficiary, and you are now married to someone else, guess what, the person you named as the beneficiary will get that money. This is not a myth. This is fact! Even if you have a will or a trust naming someone else as a beneficiary, if you listed someone directly as a beneficiary on your insurance policy form, that's who gets paid the insurance money.

Parents also make the mistake of naming their underage children as beneficiaries on their life insurance policies (usually as the back-up after the spouse). While, of course, you would want your child to get the money, the life insurance company can't cut your six-year-old a check for a million dollars. Money left to children under a life insurance policy typically triggers a court of law having to get involved and a lot of extra time, cost, and hassle. As I will explain more in the upcoming chapters, you are better off setting up a trust for your family and then naming the trust as your life insurance beneficiary, so your life insurance can go to your loved ones with the proper oversight, restrictions, and protections, and without court involvement.

As a final reminder, you should always leave your money to the person you want to benefit from your life insurance policy. Don't leave it to someone and trust that they will use it on someone else. Even if you think they would, what if they inadvertently lose it because they get sued or pass away? And again, I will show you in the upcoming chapters how setting up a trust can ensure the people you want to benefit from your life insurance will do so, and how to have someone you trust in charge of that.

LONG-TERM CARE/DISABILITY

Did you know you are six times more likely to become disabled than to have an early death? I don't know if that should make us all feel better or worse. Neither scenario is ideal. But we know the potential is there for any of us to develop a disability or get seriously injured and need daily assistance. We hope this does not happen, but if it did, we would be glad to have insurance for that.

When uncovered parents get disabled or seriously ill, it not only devastates them physically and emotionally, it also drains their finances. Therapies, treatments, and daily assistance costs a lot of money, and many times a disability or serious illness can prevent us from working like we are now. This is where Long-term care insurance or disability coverage come into play. They are policies that you buy so that you would still have income if you had to quit your job because you became disabled, sick, or needed daily assistance with activities.

Ideally, you should secure disability insurance now, during your working years, so it would provide you income if you could no longer work because of a disability or illness. You will want to make sure you understand your policy, as some disability policies only kick in if you cannot work at all, while others kick in if you don't have the physical or mental ability to perform your current specific job. For example, a surgeon who gets early onset Parkinson's might be able to work, but not work as a surgeon. You should secure a disability policy that pays out if you cannot perform your actual current job.

Long-term care insurance is typically something you secure later on. I am only putting it on your radar because, if it felt like the age of forty snuck up on us, I heard that sixty comes even sooner (which is the typical age you secure a Long-term insurance policy). Long-term care insurance means that an insurance company will help pay for your daily care or assistance if you cannot live independently (while health insurance covers your medical costs). I highly recommend we get this insurance when the time comes, as I have seen too many seniors get wiped out financially paying for out-of-pocket care costs.

LLC/CORPS

We spend so much time thinking that a misfortune—like a flood, or illness, or even death—can threaten our financial security. Far too often, we overlook the possibility of financial ruin due to the actions of other people, or something we did ourselves.

Lawsuits are an everyday part of life, unfortunately. If you are caught up in one, I hope you can get out of it quickly. It causes an emotional drain on normal people (sadly, some other people feed on contention), and the only people who really "win" are the lawyers who often fuel the fire. At one point I was so disheartened by our judicial system and our lawsuit-happy society that I almost quit practicing law! I hope you will never have to step foot in a courtroom.

So, how can you protect your family from a lawsuit? Sadly, you cannot. Anyone can sue you for anything, any day of the week, and there is not much you can do to prevent that. However, you can protect your assets from being taken by a lawsuit through asset protection measures.

One popular way to protect certain assets like your family business or your rental property is to form a corporation or a limited liability corporation (LLC). That way, if you get sued for something related to your business or rental property, they can only go after the assets that are in your corporation or LLC rather than all your personal assets like your home or personal investments.

For those of you in a field like mine where you are personally liable even if you have an LLC or corporation (like law, medicine, or therapy) make sure you also have proper malpractice insurance in place. There are lots of additional asset protection options beyond LLCs and corporations, and you should talk with your estate planning attorney if you have large sums of money at risk.

LEGAL CONTRACTS

So often, we leave our families at financial risk because we don't have the right legal contracts in place. For example, we start a business with a friend through a handshake deal only to have fights over the profits down the road without a legal agreement in place. Or maybe we lent money to a family member or friend, and they never paid us back. Or perhaps our boss promised us a bonus, but we failed to get it in writing.

Too many of us are engaging in activities where a legal agreement should be in place. Legal agreements can ensure everyone has a clear understanding of how things should play out, especially when a problem arises or there is a dispute. If you have doubt over whether a legal agreement is necessary for your specific situation, you should absolutely ask a lawyer and make sure your family is protected.

UMBRELLA POLICIES

Umbrella policies are basically insurance policies that cover anything that all your other policies do not. For example, maybe you had auto insurance and got in an accident, but your policy only covered so much. That's when an umbrella policy would cover the rest. Or maybe you had malpractice insurance for your job, but you got sued for more than your coverage. That's when an umbrella policy would kick in and pay.

The reason most families do not have an umbrella policy is because they are expensive. You and your financial advisor or estate planning attorney should determine your risks and finances to determine if an umbrella policy is worth the premiums.

MARRIAGE COUNSELING

Why would I lump marriage counseling in with all these other legal protections? It's simple: a divorce is the biggest legal threat to your assets, and absent a very strong prenuptial agreement in your favor, a divorce can cost you 50 percent of everything you own, as it typically gets divided when a couple divorces. Not only do you lose 50 percent of your assets, you also lose future assets if you are ordered to pay ongoing spousal support or child support.

WEAR YOUR SEATBELT

Hopefully, I am leaving you with a better understanding of how you can protect your assets through proper insurance, asset protection, and legal agreements. Just like you wear your seat belt to protect yourself from a hit, you need to have these protections in place to stay safe.

We can't blanket ourselves in bubble wrap and never leave the home. The truth is we can only insure and protect ourselves so much. But I hope you will sleep better at night knowing that you've done what you can.

9

CREATING A FAMILY
ESTATE PLAN

HOPEFULLY, I GOT YOU NICE and excited about your future in the Plan section of the book, and now I may seem like a real pessimist to bring up the topic of your death. I know it's a terrible thought, but because I am an estate planning lawyer, I have to make sure that all those amazing life milestones you are planning for and all the wealth you are building doesn't get ripped away from your family if something should happen to you.

I'm here to help you understand the legal and practical steps you must take to protect yourself, your loved ones, your assets, and even your legacy if anything should happen to you. Now, don't freak out at this thought. While I am not a psychic, statistically, you will live until you are very old, hopefully so old you land on *Today* with a televised shout-out when you hit your 100th!

Most parents spend so much energy building their finances, only to leave everything at risk if anything should happen to them. Did you know that 70 percent of us parents do not have our will or trust set up or a legal document designating guardians to raise our kids if something happened to us?[38]

Not shocked? Neither are many of the families who come to my workshops or work with me directly. I guess we can all find some odd sense of comfort knowing so many of us have put this most important task off or are unsure of what protections must be put in place.

Now it's time to get very uncomfortable!

If a family has not done their own legal planning to protect themselves, their assets, and their children, then when a parent gets sick or passes away, the state where they reside steps in with its own default plan to handle that for them. That's good, right? Through our state governments, 100 percent of us already have an estate plan! . . . Not good at all. That state default plan? You are not going to like it!

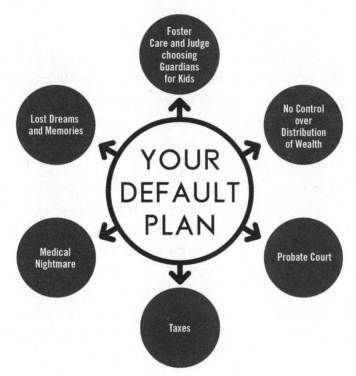

This default chart shows all the areas of your life that will have to be dealt with if you become incapacitated or die. When you fail to make plans for these areas in your life, your state will step in and clean up your mess.

Your state's default plan for your family could subject your loved ones to years of courtrooms and lawyers, determine everything from who should raise your kids to who should control your money, and even decide whether you can be kept on artificial life support if you're in a vegetative state. And while there are a lot of things the state will have to do for you that you won't like, there are also a lot of things they just won't do for you—which is even worse—such as preserve your legacy; protect your money from lawsuits, predators, and creditors; and make sure your kids don't blow all their inheritance at eighteen.

If you want to know if your state's plan is a good one or not, just ask someone who lost a loved one and had to turn to the state to clean up their affairs. They would do anything to go back in time and have their loved one create an estate plan. Leaving it to the government to handle truly is a nightmare, and knowing their process could have been completely avoided had they done their own planning makes it all the worse.

Avoid the state by setting up a proper estate plan that is designed to fully meet the needs of your young family. I am going to show you exactly what a comprehensive estate plan looks like, and how to go about creating one for your unique family. This will give you a lot of peace of mind and save your family a lot of time, money, and heartache.

PROTECTING YOUR KIDS

Parents think of ourselves as great at protecting our kids. We keep a close eye on them at the park, we make sure the stove is off, and lock the doors at night. We make sure our children are rarely exposed to anything or anyone who could harm them.

Good stuff, but it's simply not enough. Most of us have not yet taken the financial and legal steps necessary to protect our children if anything should happen to us—their protectors. We're leaving our children at great risk of harm.

When Josh and I bought our family home, the previous owner invited us to stop by the week before to show us some nuances of the property. He showed us many safety systems and precautions he'd taken to keep his family safe, including strategically placed fire extinguishers so they could extinguish flames to get to one another. He also showed us the elaborate alarm system for the home—flood lights, motion sensors, alarm bells, alarm signs, basically everything short of having an actual guard stationed inside. I remember thinking, wow, either this dad is serious about protecting his daughters, or he does not trust these teenage girls' boyfriends.

Interestingly, when we signed the final papers, we noticed on the paperwork that the home was not owned by a family trust but instead in the father's name, signaling that this father had never set up an estate plan for his family. It meant that, should anything happen to him, the home would be subject to a long and expensive court process known as probate, rather than going directly to provide support for the four daughters. His incapacity or death was a scenario the father may not have considered, or maybe he'd just put off addressing it.

How many of us are like this devoted father, going to great extremes to protect our children but overlooking some of the basic legal and financial protections our children need if anything should happen to us? It's time to look at what really happens to our kids if something happens to us so we can do something about it.

Your State's Default Plan for Your Children's Care

Most states have laws in place that provide children can be placed into temporary foster care if the parents cannot care for them (through incapacitating illness or death). A judge will then choose a guardian for any minor child who does not have one. It's the last thing we parents would want for our kids if we got sick or passed away!

There was a family in San Diego several years ago in which the parents were killed in a car accident, leaving behind three young children. Rather than those children immediately being placed in the care of extended family, they were placed in the care of strangers while for more than a year the children's two aunts battled in court over who the judge should choose as their new guardian. Can you imagine how much pain that entire family went through, especially those three young children, on top of the terrible loss of the parents?

If you don't put your own legal plans in place for the care of your children during an illness, injury, or death, the state has to step in and do that for you, and it's not an easy, overnight process. And the state's ultimate decision may not be what you as the parents would want.

The good news is that the state allows you to prevent this from happening if you sign legal paperwork designating who you would want to raise your child or children if something happened to you, and who you would want to care for them during a short term emergency, as well.

Naming Permanent Guardian for Your Kids

If you don't legally name them, permanent guardians—the long-term guardians who would raise your kids if anything should happen to you—will be chosen by a judge who most likely doesn't know you or your family. The process is often drawn out over a year full of conflict, tears, courtrooms, and lawyers, and it often pits the maternal grandparents and the paternal grandparents against one another, since they—by default—are the first potential guardians a judge would consider in many States.

If you don't like the thought of such hardship for your family, and I know you don't, then you need to legally name permanent guardians for your children. A permanent guardian can be a family member, friend, godparent, colleague, or someone else you know, love, and trust, who is willing to be legally responsible for raising your children.

Just telling your sister in conversation that you would want her as a guardian is not enough. An email to your parents before you head out the door on a kid-free getaway is not enough. Telling your spouse you would never want their mother to raise the kids is not enough! You must make it official.

Most states allow you to name permanent guardians though a stand-alone legal document that you sign in front of witness, or through your will. You will need to consult with a reputable estate planning lawyer, as we'll talk about in the Players section, who can advise you on the specific rules and requirements for your state.

I understand as a parent myself how hard it is to choose a permanent guardian for your child. There are so many things to consider, and you and your spouse may or may not agree. I have a few thoughts and tricks to help you make the absolute best decision, and to help you and your spouse get on the same page. If you and your child's other legal parent cannot agree or you aren't together anymore, you can both individually nominate who you would want in your own separate legal paperwork. If you should both pass away at the same time, a judge would consider both your nominations and choose.

Easy Three-Step Process for Choosing Permanent Guardians

To help you identify who would be a great choice to raise your kids, here is an easy three-step process my clients and workshop guests go through. You can do it right now. This process comes from estate planning guru Ali Katz and her program Personal Family Lawyer that I belonged to for many years.

I've found that this process helps clients have more clarity when making a final decision on permanent guardians. Furthermore, as you take the steps listed below, I'd urge you to focus solely on who makes the most sense as your kids' guardians for the next three years; trying to peer into the distant future to see how lives may pan out tends to be too difficult and frustrating.

STEP ONE

Take out a blank piece of paper and write down all the potential people who love your children and could potentially serve as guardians, like grandparents, aunts and uncles, cousins, adult siblings, friends, or coworkers. Ideally, you will write down at least five to seven names. If you have one or more couples in mind (i.e., your brother and his wife), then write both of their names together on the list for now.

Now this is not the time to be evaluating people or shooting down names your partner suggests. All you are doing here is making a list of potential guardians who could potentially raise your kids.

STEP TWO

Put away your list of potential people and take out a separate blank piece of paper. Write down a list of your top three qualities or characteristics you would want in a person who is raising your children (i.e., age of guardian, religion, lifestyle, location of guardian, or integrity). I like to identify these qualities as the "non-negotiables," meaning you will not compromise on these criteria.

One thing you should never consider is the financial resources of the potential guardian. As we talked about back in the insurance section, it is *our* responsibility to leave behind either enough assets or enough life insurance to raise our kids. You can, of course, consider the financial *integrity* of your guardians, since your kids will see what behaviors, financial and others, are modeled for them.

STEP THREE

Compare the first sheet that lists your potential guardians and the second sheet that lists your priorities. Rank in order the "potential people" you listed, from top choice down to last choice, based on who offers or possesses most, if not all, of your top three priorities. Do you see some names emerge to the top now?

While this simple three-step process is not magic, it does help you look at things objectively.

Six Common Mistakes Parents Make When Choosing Guardians

When you formalize your legal wishes for guardianship, make sure you avoid the six common mistakes that most parents and their lawyers make when they set it all up. Here's another gem of a list I picked up when training under Ali Katz's program:

MISTAKE #1: NOT BEING BOTH OBJECTIVE AND SUBJECTIVE WHEN PICKING GUARDIANS

Think back to when you fell in love with your spouse; and now think back to when you decided to get married. The first was probably all emotion. The second, I bet, was an emotional *and* logical decision. You knew you felt a deep, passionate connection, but you also evaluated character, qualities, values, and what type of life you would build together.

Similarly, when it comes to choosing guardians for our kids, we should not only think about who we love and their relationship with our children, but also evaluate their qualities and values and the type of life they can actually provide for our children.

I remember talking with one couple who were at odds over guardianship. The wife wanted to name her parents, and the husband, who had been raised by his single mom, felt he'd be deeply betraying his mom if he did not choose her as the permanent guardian. The husband's emotions were really affecting his decision. And even though his mom would have been a *great* choice, I'm not sure he or his wife believed she would be the *best* choice.

His was a heart versus head conflict. He said, "I don't want her to feel like she is losing something," mindful that she had experienced great loss in her past.

Many times, our emotions and loyalty to those we love can overpower our decision making when choosing a permanent guardian. It's normal. But keep in mind that you are not taking anything away from someone you love by choosing to make someone else a guardian. You are simply choosing not to add an additional role on top of the special role they already have in your child's life.

If you stick with the easy three-step process and make sure not to let your emotions disproportionately control your decision, you will be making an emotional *and* logical decision when choosing who is best for the permanent guardianship role.

MISTAKE #2: NOT NAMING AN HEIR AND A SPARE

Notice how most royal families have an "heir" and a "spare," and that they never travel together? If something happened to the first in line to the throne, they need to have a backup so the line will continue.

We may not be royals, but there is something significant we can learn from the heir and spare concept when it comes to setting up guardianship. You need to make sure you have designated backup guardians just in case your first choice can't do it or declines to serve. I usually suggest couples list two backup guardians.

MISTAKE #3: NAMING COUPLES WITHOUT CONDITIONS

Ideally, you would list a person or a couple, and if something in their life changed, or if something unexpectedly happened to them, you would just update your guardianship wishes. But there could be some serious complicating circumstances.

For example, what if you picked your mom and dad to serve as guardians, but your mom and you were killed in an accident together? Would you still want your dad to serve alone, or would you rather have your sister, who was your second choice, for guardian? Such circumstantial choices need to be made clear before disaster strikes.

Or what if you picked your brother and sister-in-law, but they were no longer married at the time of your death? Do you still want both of them, or maybe just your brother alone, or neither at all? Again, you need to make the decision under such conditions clear.

Maybe you really want your in-laws as guardians, but only if they will raise the kids in your hometown. This needs to be made clear.

Some attorneys will tell you not to name a couple at all in case one cannot serve or the couple divorces. A simple remedy is to name a couple, but to also address your wishes for common circumstances such as death or divorce, that could result in one or both of them not being able to serve.

When discussing conditions for guardianship, a client once said to me, "Well, I really want my sister, but can I make it a condition that she divorces her husband first?" No, but it opened up a great conversation about whether she really wanted her kids to be raised in his home if she is so opposed to his being a guardian. Make sure you and your attorney talk through any unique conditions you may have to consider or requirements you have, and discuss whether you can or should legally include them when identifying a guardian.

MISTAKE #4: HAVING THE GUARDIANS MANAGE YOUR CHILDREN'S MONEY

Sometimes, the person you choose to raise your children in your absence is also the best person to manage the money you left behind for them. But this is not always the case.

Raising children and managing money are different skills. Your spouse may be the most hands-on parent in the world, but may not be the best person when it comes to making investments. Or maybe your spouse is great at making money but not so great at arranging the children's birthday parties.

When you choose a couple to serve as guardian, hopefully between the two of them, they are the best choice to raise the kids *and* manage the money. But what if they aren't?

You might want to ensure that there is money-management oversight applied—someone to officially look over the shoulder of your guardian.

I like to assume the best about people, and I'm sure you do, too, but assigning your guardians to also manage money is something that should not be done lightly. In many cases, it makes a lot of sense to leave the money management to a different family member or an outside professional or institution who is really good at doing just that—managing money.

MISTAKE #5: NOT EXCLUDING GUARDIANS

One of the most difficult parts of my job is sitting down with a couple, discussing guardianship, and discovering why someone in the extended family is *not* being considered for guardianship. In some cases, the situation is so severe that we actually recommend that person be excluded from ever being considered as a guardian.

You may be wondering why someone you clearly did not pick to be the guardian could end up being appointed by a judge, especially when you have already identified several other people that you would want to serve as guardian.

It happens in the rare cases when guardianship is contested, the guardians you wanted declined or have died, or a judge concluded it was not in your child's best interest to be placed with them. In any of those scenarios, a judge begins looking within the family to find a suitable permanent guardian for your children.

In most states, judges give preference to your parents and your spouse's parents and would have to choose between them. If that process is unsuccessful, the judge will start looking at your siblings or your spouse's siblings. And this is why it's imperative that, in addition to naming who you want to serve as your permanent guardian, you also exclude anyone in your family that you would never want a judge to consider.

I recall sitting in my office with a couple when the wife broke down in tears as she painfully explained to me why her mom should never be considered as the guardian of her children. I also recall a husband apathetically reference his biological dad when asked if anyone should be excluded. He said something along the lines of, "Yeah, knowing him, he'd show up for once if money was somehow involved."

These are sad situations, and my heart goes out to people who have to exclude a guardian. I also admire and am inspired by people who, despite their unfair upbringing, have gone on to enjoy healthy lives and create the families they always deserved.

You should feel confident that there is a very delicate and confidential way to accomplish guardianship exclusion. The excluded person would never find out unless the guardianship you had set up was contested and a judge had to start from scratch.

MISTAKE #6: NOT LEAVING BEHIND INSTRUCTIONS AND OTHER IMPORTANT INFORMATION

We've all heard the expression that *kids don't come with an instruction manual.* All of us parents have had to learn on the job. We've had to learn through others' examples, and plenty of trial and error, how to meet our children's needs and build a positive world for them.

Inheriting kids, though, is different. They've already had a life before being placed with you, and they have just come through something very traumatic. Obviously, parents should do everything possible in advance to ensure a successful transition. This is why you really should have an instruction manual for raising your kids! I'm serious.

At our firm we call this document "Instructions to Guardians," and it is a key way to ensure that your guardians understand your children's needs, beliefs, and support systems, and your goals for each child. Believe me—your guardians would really appreciate some kind of guidance so they can raise your kids, honor your wishes, and make sure they are meeting what you have laid out as their emotional, physical, spiritual, and intellectual needs.

A key component to these instructions is guidance on relationships. What relationships are important to your children and how do you want your guardians to help foster them? For example, continuing to see grandparents may be on your list. You would think this is a no-brainer, but your guardians have their own lives, too, and time gets tight, so you need to spell out to your guardians exactly what is important to you. You don't want your wishes to be unclear; you don't want relatives turning to the court system to continue to have access to your children. Set your vision from the get-go so that, before your guardians even consent to serving as guardians, they know what the expectations are.

I hope that you feel a huge step closer to naming permanent guardians for your kids. Let me encourage you not to leave your kids at risk one more day. Make a commitment with yourself and your spouse that you will make this decision right away.

The Temporary Care of Your Children (Avoiding Foster Care)

Remember the family in San Diego whose three children were temporarily placed in the care of strangers after their parents died? I know it's the last thing you would want for your kids.

It's not enough to think about who your children's permanent guardian should be. You should plan for a short-term guardian who could care for them until the permanent guardians can arrive. Since your permanent guardian may not be immediately available or may live out of state, you need someone local who can step in temporarily.

I recommend that parents name at least four or five temporary guardians in case one or more are not available to help. Temporary guardians should live within twenty minutes of your home so they can quickly get to the children during an emergency. You should sign a legal document with your estate planning attorney designating these people as temporary guardians, and then send them a copy of the paperwork in case they need to show it to state authorities. You also should make sure you leave instructions for caregivers and keep the information in your wallet for first responders so they would know who to contact in an emergency.

Medical Directives for Your Children

When we were growing up and our parents took a trip, they would write a little note saying that whoever we were staying with could get treatment for us at the hospital if we got hurt. But today, most hospitals require far more than a written note. They require that you complete a medical directive for your children if you want to authorize someone other than you to make medical decisions for your child in an emergency.

A few years ago in Los Angeles, a husband and wife were killed in a car accident on a busy freeway. Their daughter was in the car with them and was seriously injured. She was rushed to a local hospital and immediately placed under the care of Child Protective Services. Several major medical procedures were performed on her, all at the direction of strangers who had no idea what the parents' wishes were for their daughter's treatment or care.

Wouldn't you rather have a trusted family member or friend—rather than a complete stranger—make medical decisions for your child if you could not? Completing a medical directive for your child can ensure such decisions would be made by who you want and how you want.

Also, once your child hits age eighteen, you no longer have the legal authority to make medical decisions for them. Before you send them off to college, make sure they complete their own medical directive (a.k.a. an Advanced Health Care Directive) so you, or whoever they choose, can make emergency medical decisions for them if they cannot.

Let me encourage you to please get all these protections for your kids right away. I know for all of us parents coming through a major health pandemic together, we understand how quickly things can change and how fragile life can be. Make sure your kids are protected no matter what, so that you can have that peace of mind.

PROTECTING YOUR MONEY

If we want to make sure our family is taken care of no matter what, then we need protect our assets, making them available for their support if anything should happen to us. I have seen so many families spend their lifetime building wealth, only to lose so much of it when they die because they had not secured their money and had to go through the court system.

The saddest calls I get as an estate planning attorney are from family members who just lost a spouse or parent, only to realize they will have to go through a very painful, long, and expensive court process because the right legal plans were not in place.

Your State's Default Plan for Your Money

Without documented legal plans to pass money to your family when you die, the state will step in and do it for you. Generally speaking, any assets or accounts that you own jointly with your spouse will automatically go to them upon your death. Your spouse is most likely (but not always) considered co-owner of those assets or accounts. Also, if you've named a beneficiary on your life insurance policy or on your retirement account, that money typically gets paid out directly to whoever you designated.

But as we are aware, not everyone dies in perfect order, and sometimes even both spouses pass away. Not everyone owns everything jointly with a spouse, either. Many of us are single parents, or perhaps have blended families. And eventually, the surviving spouse who got the money will die. And that's exactly why your state has something called Probate Court, where the government steps in and decides how your assets get passed on when you've neglected to properly plan for this yourself.

Your assets and money must go through Probate to get to someone else when you die. While the process of probate varies from state to state, I'll be focusing on what probate is like here in California, where we are notorious for having one of the most convoluted and expensive probate processes in the country.

Keep in mind that each state specifies how much money and assets you must have to be subject to probate, which in most cases is not much. For example, currently, in California, you need only a little more than $160,000 in assets to be subject to probate.

Here's what your family could experience if they must go through probate to get your assets or money if you pass away without having plans in place:

- A very long process—it often lasts two years or more.
- Your money being frozen and not immediately accessible for your children.
- An open and public court process, meaning anyone can go down to the court and see exactly what and how much you owned at the time of your death. (That's why, if a celebrity's family has to go through court, we can see what that celebrity owned upon their death.)
- The responsibility of opening up your estate's probate landing on someone else's shoulders. They are stuck cleaning up your mess. Imagine that—you die unexpectedly and your family not only has to deal with your loss, but also gets thrown into the court system for several years.
- An extremely depressing experience for your loved ones. Most courtrooms are depressing, but probate is packed with grieving families.
- Grievances and arguments. Probate court is a platform for your family members to publicly vent and battle it out over your children or estate.
- And finally, a very, very (and I mean VERY) expensive experience.

Let's focus more on that last characteristic—just how much money probate can cost your family.

The Financial Cost of Probate

The cost of probate varies depending on the state you live in and oftentimes depending on the size of your estate. In California, for example, the probate code sets the cost for probate as a percentage of the total estate value. This percentage pays the attorney, the person administering your estate, and court fees. We estimate for our clients that probate will cost them about 5 percent of their total estate worth (it could be less or more depending on the size and complexity of your estate).

This is when parents will often say: "I don't own much. The bank basically owns my home and I've barely paid down the mortgage. I have a lot of student loans still and my retirement account doesn't have a lot in it. I have a life insurance policy, but that just goes to my spouse, and then to my kids, right?"

If only.

Let me give you a simple scenario to help explain what probate could cost a family. Let's say two parents with young children pass away without any legal plans in place. Someone will need to step up and open a probate through the court to get the money and assets to their kids. Let's say this is what the parents owned when they died:

Home: $750,000 (value)
Bank and Savings Accounts: $15,000 checking account, $30,000 savings account.
Stock: $15,000
Retirement Accounts: $120,000 combined.
Life Insurance: $1,250,000 combined.
Debt: $400,000 mortgage; $60,000 student loans; $30,000 cars; and $15,000 credit cards.

Now when I look at this scenario, I see a lot of debt. I wish this family had read the Plan section of this book! But debt-ridden is not how the probate court sees this family when they calculate how much probate will cost. That's because probate court doesn't factor in your debt when they calculate your probate fees. The court bases the fees on the fair market value of your estate:

ASSET	FAIR Market Value
Home	$750,000
Checking and Savings	$45,000
Stock	$15,000
Retirement Accounts*	$120,000
Combined Life Insurance*	$1,250,000
Total Estate Worth:	$2,180,000
	—(nothing; court will not count the debt.)
Probate Cost (at 5%)	$109,000

That's crazy, right? The probate cost for this recently deceased couple is $109,000.

Even if the retirement policies and the life insurance policies had named the kids as back-up beneficiaries, because they are minors the money from the policies can end up in the probate case. Once the probate case has closed, whatever money is left after all costs are paid gets placed into accounts for each child, and the adult in charge of the money must file accountings every other year with the court to show how the money is being spent. Once the kids hit eighteen, boom, they get the money outright without any restrictions or protections.

I recall a probate nightmare from my hometown city in which a young boy's parents passed away, and families from his school felt compelled to collect money to help buy him clothing and shoes because the parents' money was tied up in a convoluted probate court process. Families don't realize how grueling the probate

* Normally, retirement accounts and life insurance policies avoid probate because you can name a direct beneficiary for those policies, but if the beneficiary is a minor child, those policies get incorporated into the probate case.

process can be and how long it can last. The probate system leaves family members who were dependent on parents being unable to get immediate support for their needs. Probate court is not like a drive-through ATM where someone can just stop by and order cash the moment the child you left behind needs it.

Are you leaving your family at risk of a terrible scenario like this? By not planning, or by having poor planning, are you subjecting your family to the expense and hassle and heartache of probate? I know you love your family and care about them so much. Please don't leave them at risk of probate. You need to take the legal steps necessary to avoid it!

How a Revocable Living Trust Avoids Probate and Protects Money

The way you avoid the grueling process of probate is by setting up a revocable living trust. A trust is a legal document—created with your estate planning attorney—that says this is who we are, this is who we love, this is how we wish to pass our money to our loved ones (with any conditions or protections), and this is who is in charge of making this all happen (an adult you trust). A revocable living trust, when set up correctly, is basically opting out of your state's Probate process so your assets can quickly and efficiently support those you leave behind.

Most families think all they need to avoid probate is a will. That is absolutely not true. A will does not avoid probate, but instead simply tells a judge how you want your assets to be distributed and who should oversee that (i.e. a named family member or friend). A will is important for other reasons, like naming guardians, but is not the best method for passing your assets to your family.

ASSET PROTECTION TRUST OPTION FOR YOUR SPOUSE

When you leave money to your spouse in a trust, you can decide to leave it to them outright (so it's completely theirs), or in a spousal asset protection trust with restrictions and protections.

When you leave your money outright to your spouse, your share when you die goes straight to them and they are then free to do whatever they wish with it—give it away to a new spouse, leave it to children from a prior or future relationship who are not yours, donate it, spend it, or anything else. They also are not obligated to leave it upon their death to the children you had together; they retain the right to change the beneficiary whenever they want. The money can also be taken from them down the road if they are sued, or by a future creditor, predator, or divorce from a subsequent spouse.

Some spouses don't like that the money they leave their spouse would have no restrictions or protections. It's not that they do not trust their spouse, they just don't trust what could happen in life or third parties who might come along and take the money that was intended to stay in the family—their spouse's future creditor, predators, spouse, or whomever.

The good news is that you can structure your trust with an asset protection election, so you can still leave your spouse your money when you pass away but protect it from any future third parties or risks. This protection is also popular with families who are blended and want to ensure children from other relationships would get money after their step-parent passes away, rather than risk that it gets lost through the step-parent intentionally or unintentionally. Surviving parents who work in professions where the risk of being sued is high—like physicians or lawyers—like this protected structure as well, so they know that in the future if they get sued, they would only have their personal assets at risk, and not their late spouse's trust since it is protected in trust.

ASSET PROTECTION TRUST OPTION FOR YOUR CHILD

Asset protection can extend to your children as well. Their inheritance can be kept in trust for their lifetime, so it's always safeguarded from any ill-intentioned people who may come along, or from a divorce, creditor, predator, or lawsuit. Typically, when parents elect to asset protect money for a child through a trust, they let the child—upon reaching a certain age of maturity— manage the trust so they aren't being controlled from the grave but are still financially protected from any future harm.

I had a client who received a half million dollars when she turned eighteen because of the death of a relative. Once that check was cut, she said she took a long vacation instead of going on to college as she had planned. That "vacation" lasted for several years, until she found herself unexpectedly pregnant. After the birth of her son, she came to see me for help to set up her trust. I told her she didn't need one. Why? Because she had no money left. The money that was meant to enable her future sabotaged it instead, because it was not properly protected. Had the money she received gone to her through a trust with the right restrictions and protections, she would have been spared a lot of heartache and pain.

IF YOU HAVE A CHILD WITH SPECIAL NEEDS

One more option I want to put on the radar for those of you who have a child with special needs is to make sure whatever you leave them when you pass away is done through a special needs trust. This is the best way to leave that child money without it jeopardizing any government benefits they may qualify for when they are an adult, as a special needs trust is exempt from the income and asset requirements of Social Security's Supplemental Security Income program (SSI).

A special needs trust allows you to leave them money that can help supplement their care costs, on top of the government benefits they receive. It's a wonderful way to ensure that their quality of life will continue if anything happens to you. You can designate a legal adult you trust to help manage the money for your child and see that their needs are met. Not all estate planning attorneys are trained to set up these types of trusts, so you will need to find a special needs trust attorney who can help.

CONNECTING YOUR ASSETS TO YOUR TRUST

Once your trust is signed, you must connect your assets to it. Most people who try to set up a trust online without the help of the lawyer skip this step, and then their family is devastated to find out their trust did not work. For example, if you own your home in your own name, now you will own it in the name of your trust. You are free to continue to sell things or buy things as long as you are alive and mentally capable, but once you pass away, whatever assets are connected to the trust will pass on according to the terms of your trust and avoid probate.

It's important to make sure that you check your assets every year—your bank accounts, your life insurance policies, your retirement accounts, and more—to make sure they are properly connected to your trust. That's because any assets that are not properly connected to your trust upon your death could end up having to go through probate.

CREATING YOUR REVOCABLE LIVING TRUST

So why aren't we all rushing out to get a trust as part of a comprehensive estate plan for our family? I don't know. Probably the same reason we are not rushing to clean out the garage. It seems like a daunting and overwhelming task that we would rather put off while we spend our time and money on other things.

But now that you really know how much your spouse and children are at risk, please don't put this off for one more second.

THE FAMILY NEST EGG

Take action to protect your loved ones and your assets, and get your trust in place. Avoiding probate for your family and safeguarding your money is entirely in your hands.

PROTECTING YOURSELF

Part of the estate planning process during which you put together the guardianship for the kids and set up a trust also includes creating important medical directives to protect you and provide guidance if you are seriously hurt.

When I was out walking with one of my sons a few years ago, I received a call on my cell phone from a longtime friend whom I had not heard from in years. I can still clearly remember standing on the side of my neighborhood's main road with my son in his stroller, processing what she was saying to me for what felt like an eternity. She skipped the "Hi, how are you" part and began with, "I don't know if you heard, but Joe* was in a very bad accident." My heart sank. "It's very serious," she continued. "The doctors are talking to me about removing him from life support. I don't know what to do." Her husband was in his late thirties. Their son was just a little boy. They were normal people just like you and me. And, in a flash, due to a serious accident, their lives were forever changed.

You may remember the very public case of Terri Schiavo. She was a beautiful young woman who had a heart attack that caused major damage to her brain due to a lack of oxygen. After two and a half months in a coma, her doctors labeled her condition a "persistent vegetative state." Terri Schiavo did not have any medical directives in place stating what she would want to have happen to her in that situation. Sadly, her husband and her parents did not agree on whether she should be artificially kept alive, and for *fifteen* years they battled in court over whether she should be removed from life support.

Have you left your spouse or your loved ones in a situation where they would not have a legal document to turn to regarding your wishes? It's imperative for you to make your medical wishes known.

How to Make Your Medical Wishes Known

My friend's situation and public cases like Terri Schiavo's show just how important it is to make our medical wishes known. There are three main documents you will need: a living will, an advanced health care directive, and a HIPAA authorization. Sometimes, all three of these are together on one form. The important thing is to make sure all three components are covered, whether in one or multiple forms.

LIVING WILL

A living will is a legal declaration you sign in front of a witness or notary (depending on your state's requirements) that states what you want to have happen if you are on life support and the doctors have determined you will not recover. For women, you can also address what those wishes would be in that case if you also were pregnant and the baby could eventually be born and live a healthy life.

It's important for you to make your wishes clear and documented. Telling your family is not enough. There are too many emotions in a tragic life-support scenario, and everyone will have their own feelings and opinions. During the COVID-19 crisis, we have seen physicians and family members engaged in this kind of tragedy as most patients do not have a living will and were being placed on ventilators. Adding to the stress and challenge was the common practice of closing hospitals to outside visitors, making communication with family and determining the patient's wishes extremely difficult.

ADVANCED HEALTH CARE DIRECTIVE

An Advanced Health Care Directive (also known as a Health Care Power of Attorney) works in conjunction with your living will and allows you to designate someone to make and carry out your medical decisions for you if you are incapacitated. It provides instructions on your medical evaluation and treatment, long-term care and hospice, your wishes on staying in your residence versus being placed in a facility, who can hire and fire your doctors, and your wishes when it comes to pain relief, psychiatric treatment, organ donation, and more.

Don't leave your family in a position where it's unclear who your medical decision maker should be. Maybe you *think* it would be obvious that you want your spouse, but what if your spouse couldn't do it? What if your spouse was also injured or was simply not in a mental state to make decisions for you when needed? An Advanced Health Care Directive addresses all these scenarios, and every person needs one.

HIPAA AUTHORIZATION

You probably already know that your medical information is private. If I called your doctor and asked for a copy of your latest medical exam, they'd tell me to take a hike. Congress passed a law known as the Health Insurance Portability and Accountability Act (HIPAA) that limits use, disclosure, or release of your health information.

It makes sense that a stranger should not be able to call your doctor and get sensitive medical information about you, but what if it's your best friend and they had just rushed down to the hospital because they heard you had been in an accident. Shouldn't they be able to at least find out what happened to you?

The answer is no, unless you have authorized them to receive that type of information in an emergency situation by signing a

HIPAA Authorization. That's the only legal way for hospitals to disclose your medical information to others. Typically, you will name a few key trusted family members or friends who can also help get the word out to others.

Once you sign your medical directives, make sure that your loved ones know how to find it during a medical emergency. Having it locked up in a safety deposit box where no one can access it is not helpful. Additionally, I recommend you file a copy with your primary care physician and your local hospital. You should also bring a copy with you anytime you are going in for a major medical procedure.

Financial Power of Attorney

Beyond having medical directives to protect you in an emergency, you also need to make sure you've authorized someone who can handle your finances during that time. Typically that someone would be your spouse if you are married, or another adult you trust with money.

A Financial Power of Attorney is a legal form that allows the person you've chosen to do everything from opening up your mail, to paying your bills, providing money to your kids, managing your property, or any other pressing financial needs you cannot complete if you are seriously ill and mentally incapable.

When a parent has not taken time to do this, the family potentially has to go through a court process to get what is called a conservatorship, so they can handle these matters during an incapacity. It is the last thing families want to be dealing with when a loved one is in the hospital. Take the time to complete a financial power of attorney, and make sure it is accessible if needed.

PROTECTING YOUR LEGACY

As parents we can get so focused on making sure our families will always be protected and provided for that, when we go to set up an estate plan, we overlook preserving the most important "asset" of all—which is ourselves.

Think about the special memories and dreams for your children that might get lost if something happened to you. Your family will keep memories alive, so to speak, but how would they know what was *truly* in your heart?

A couple years ago, I helped a husband and wife do the responsible thing and set up their estate plan, making sure each other and their young kids would be taken care of "just in case." Well "just in case" happened a few months later when the husband found out he was dying of a very aggressive form of cancer.

One of the things the couple had done when we worked together was record a legacy interview, capturing in audio (some parents choose video) their answers to questions about their favorite memories, their kids, their advice, their views, and their love for their family. He had no idea at the time of the recording he would not live to see his children grow up.

In the recording, the husband talks about each of his very young children in detail, what he loved about them, their personalities, and what made them so special and unique to him. Then he said, "The one thing about my kids is that they are strong kids, and I know that no matter what comes against them in life, they will overcome."

These young children—whose memories will fade over time—can hear their father in his very own words capture what he thought of them and how much he loved them, and hear him express his confidence in their strength. It is a treasure the entire family is blessed to have.

Could it be possible to capture your memories on audio or video—like that moment you met your spouse? Could it possible that you could be part of your child's wedding day, even if you were not here? Could it be possible to tell your child what a wonderful parent they will be the day your grandchild is born? Could it be possible to tell your spouse and children how much you love them, even if you are gone? The answer is yes, and it can be done by recording what's in your heart and soul for the people you leave behind.

The truth is that I did not get into estate planning because I had a burning desire to deal with death and talk about it all day long. I did it because I know how special our families are to us, and I want to help parents just like you make sure that you've done everything in your power to protect them and provide for them no matter what. Take the time to plan for your family, and don't forget to preserve yourself.

PUTTING AN ESTATE PLAN TOGETHER

Now that you know how important it is to have an estate plan, I'm confident that you won't leave your family at risk one more day.

We've talked about how your kids could be placed in temporary foster care, how a judge would have to choose a guardian, how your loved ones would go through a long and expensive court process known as probate, and how your kids would get money outright at eighteen, how your lack of medical directives could leave your family in the dark, and how your legacy could become lost. I know that the state's plan for your family is not what you want, and I don't want that for your family either.

Putting together an estate plan can seem overwhelming. It's not easy to choose a reputable estate planning lawyer to assist you, and it's tempting to try to use those online drafting systems that, frankly, may not even work.

I'll admit that not everyone needs to work with an attorney. And not everyone needs a trust. So many things depend on your personal and financial situation. If you own more than just personal belongings, such as a home or a life insurance policy, then I advocate that you meet with an attorney who can help guide you on what type of planning you need. Don't be fooled by online platforms that provide you cheap boilerplate documents and warn you that they are not responsible for the paperwork actually working. Get together with a reputable estate planning attorney who has a fiduciary duty to act in your best interest and is responsible for making sure it's done right.

Yes, you will find that there are a wide range of fees associated with estate planning. Before you ask any estate planning law firm what they charge, first ask them what their service includes. It's the only way to gauge their value. Also be sure to ask what charges you may incur if you need to ask a question in the future or modify your plan. In the Players section, I will share with you how to find and interview an estate planning attorney.

I know it may feel like I'm leaving you with a very big task—putting an estate plan together to protect your family. But really, is there anything more important than taking care of the people we love? Don't leave your family at risk one more day. Make the appointment with a reputable estate planning attorney today and make it happen. Know that when you leave this world (hopefully not for a very long time), you will be leaving your loved ones safe, protected, and well taken care of. Now that's a legacy to leave behind.

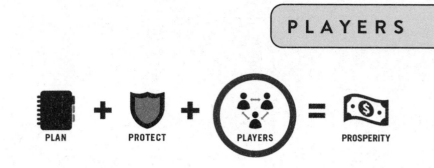

PLAN + PROTECT + PLAYERS = PROSPERITY

10

BUILDING YOUR WINNING TEAM

I HOPE I'VE BEEN SUCCESSFUL in conveying what it takes to build wealth and secure your family's future. While we all have our work cut out for us to check off those entries on our **If Life Were Perfect** list, the good news is that we do not have to go it alone. This is where building your winning team comes in!

My ten-year-old daughter, Kate, is a star on (and off) the soccer field. She is fast, fierce, and competitive, and I just love to watch her play. She has been the top scorer in her league year after year. But two years ago, she was put on a struggling team, and the coach's strategy was to holler at Kate to play the entire field. After running here, there, and everywhere, she would often tire out in the last quarter and cry that she hated soccer.

The next year everything changed. She was put on a different team with teammates up to the task of doing their jobs and an encouraging coach. Kate was freed up to focus on what she did best—scoring goals. When we went to high-five her after the first game, she was over the moon and said, "Mom, did you see how much my midfielders helped me? They helped me so much so I could score goals!"

And for us, that was the real win right there. Kate experienced an important life lesson that is easy to miss—what a difference it makes having a winning team behind you.

You cannot win your financial games all alone. Too many of us try to handle our finances without leveraging expert advice and assistance. Too many of us get distracted from focusing on what we do best. We may think we can play all the positions on our own, save money by doing it ourselves and not paying for help, or even feel self-conscious allowing others into our finances, but this only leads to burn-out and missed opportunities. We don't even realize just how much farther and faster we could have gone with a winning team behind us.

The truth is that no matter how smart we are, it is impossible for us to become experts in every single area we must succeed in to reach those goals on our **If Life Were Perfect** list. I may be an estate planning lawyer with a lot of financial knowledge, but even I have teammates—a CPA, a bookkeeper, a life insurance agent, a financial advisor, a coach, and other advisors—who help me go further and faster than I would alone. You need these players, too!

Having a winning team is about getting the objective advice and guidance that may be hard to see through your own personal filter. The worst dynamic is when one spouse is trying to be the sole player, coach, and referee on every financial decision, and then wonders why their spouse is asking to switch teams! A team of advisors can ensure shared power and help both spouses take responsibility for the family finances (even if one takes the lead on certain tasks).

Having a winning team also means backup—people besides you who can be there for your loved ones if anything unexpected should happen to you. If your family must depend on you and you alone for their tax, financial, legal, and practical advice, what happens if you get seriously ill or pass away? You will sleep better at night knowing that your spouse and children's financial security extends beyond you.

As you think about all the steps you must take right now to build wealth and secure your family's future, who do you think belongs on your winning team? While there are many players who can help us excel in life, here are the characteristics of the S.T.A.R. players every family must have for their financial journey:

S MART

Your S.T.A.R. players must be highly trained experts in their fields. You will want to find out as much as you can about where they received their education, where they have worked in the past, what special training they have received, what resources they use to help them perform their jobs, what continuing education they receive, and how they get answers to problems they have not dealt with before.

T EAM PLAYER

Your S.T.A.R. players must be willing to work with one another and communicate well for your benefit. You do not want people on your team with large egos or who feel threatened by another person's expertise. Your family's finances will require multiple areas of expertise. You need S.T.A.R. players who will stay in position while helping point you to which team member is best suited to advise in each situation. We also typically recommend you hold a team meeting with your S.T.A.R players at least once a year or when a big change is on the horizon.

A FFORDABLE

Your S.T.A.R. players must be affordable. Not necessarily the cheapest. Not the most expensive. But players who give you the best value, thus warranting their fee. Many people object to hiring outside professionals simply because they cost money. They try to reduce cost with a do-it-yourself strategy or by turning to discount professionals, not realizing that such approaches will typically cost them far more in the end than what they would have paid for the right help. If you think of the cost for your S.T.A.R players as an investment, then you can refocus on evaluating whether your gains and savings outweigh what you will spend.

R EPUTABLE

Your S.T.A.R. players must have outstanding reputations. You will want to know as much as you can about them from their peers and past clients. Beyond expertise, effectiveness, and affordability, your S.T.A.R. players must have integrity. Anyone who you allow to deal with your family and finances must be completely trustworthy. You can find out how others perceive your S.T.A.R. players by checking online reviews, researching their professional background, asking your other S.T.A.R. players for their opinion on a prospective advisor, and asking friends or family who have worked with the prospective S.T.A.R. player.

Now that you understand what qualifies a professional as a S.T.A.R player, let's take a look at which positions you will need to fill:

FINANCIAL TEACHERS

Every winning team needs S.T.A.R. financial teachers to help us understand the financial, legal, and practical steps we parents must take to build wealth and secure our family's future. Just today, my son's dentist asked me to help him with his financial and legal planning and said with a little embarrassment, "I just don't know much about these topics." I replied, "That's okay. I don't really know much about dentistry either."

Even if we had smart parents who modeled financial integrity for us, it doesn't mean we learned the ins and outs of managing and investing money. Just because we went to great schools does not mean were taught how to secure our financial future or save for our retirement (why is that by the way?). It is important for us to find those financial teachers out there who can help us on our journey.

Even if we're working with professional advisors, we should seek out voices in the financial world who can educate us about money. They can be people you personally know who are willing to share, but they can also be public figures!

Look to literature. What authors have you read and come away with new insights into managing or growing your finances? Tap into TV and podcasts. What shows and pods helped you understand a unique financial principle you had not thought about before? What other media sources do you follow to stay informed on the latest changes in the financial markets or to find practical tips for great financial moves you should be making? We are so fortunate to have free (or relatively inexpensive) access to great financial teachers.

Start adding these financial voices to your everyday life and see how much your mindset and choices will change. I mentioned earlier a couple who paid off all their student loans after the wife started listening to a finance podcast and felt motivated to eliminate debt. Try swapping out music during your morning workout, if even for ten minutes, to listen to a TED Talk. When you're driving your car, put on a finance podcast for a few minutes and hope your kids will overhear it. My kids and their friends learned all about the fifteen-year mortgage from Suze Orman on our way to grab lunch (it was one of those "hate me now, thank me later" mom moments)! Everything you learn from financial teachers can help you on your financial journey and encourage you to stay focused.

THE FINANCIAL ADVISOR

Every winning team needs a S.T.A.R. financial advisor! Your advisor helps you create a financial plan for your family and helps you invest your money. While we are ultimately responsible for the financial choices we make and must understand what our financial advisor is doing on our behalf, a financial advisor can provide expert advice and strategies that go beyond our general understanding.

Financial advisors can help you create a timeline for reaching all your financial goals. It's pretty cool how that works. You basically identify all your financial and life goals with your financial advisor, and they help put together a financial timeline and strategy to help you reach them. For example, if your goal is to retire early, the advisor will map out how much money you must be saving and investing today to reach that goal, along with recommendations on the best investment strategies to use. Or if you are wondering what to do with the 401(k) from your old job, they can advise you on your next best step.

The financial advisor also stays well-informed on the volatility of the markets and how your different investments are performing. While I enjoy keeping up with the market, I don't always know how one market is affecting another that day, or the optimal timing for me to buy or sell my stocks. The financial advisor is getting real time information constantly and evaluates your best options for you.

Your financial advisor also may help you secure life insurance for your family. While many financial advisors choose to focus on investments only, they typically have someone in their office who can help you in this regard, or refer you to a life insurance agent. It's important to ask the financial advisor if they or someone else should be helping you with that.

I have been fortunate to meet and work with a lot of financial advisors on behalf of clients, and on my own behalf. I've seen so many charts and diagrams from them over the years that at times I want to bang my head against the wall! But I know what a difference it makes having a good financial advisor on your team who you can trust and who is top of their game.

Here are the main characteristics to look for in a financial advisor when adding this S.T.A.R. player to your winning team:

1. Choose a financial advisor who focuses on planning, not products.

The best professional relationships are formed when the professional and the client have a team mentality, the professional is listening carefully to the client's goals and needs, and the professional is educating the client on their best options. You want to avoid working with someone who goes straight to pitching a product or investment that may or may not achieve your unique objectives. The number one complaint I hear from clients is that a financial advisor immediately pitched a high commission product they really did not need, or the advisor did not take time to fully understand the client's goals. People know when they are being sold something, and that is no way to begin a relationship.

2. Find out how the financial advisor gets compensated.

Not all financial advisors get paid the same way. Some get paid on a flat-fee basis, meaning you pay them a set amount of money regardless of what product or investment they select for you, or they take an annual percentage fee (usually 1 percent of the value of assets they are managing for you). Others get paid on commission and will get compensated from the product or investment they chose for you. Understanding how the advisor gets compensated is key to trust and full disclosure. Just because a financial advisor gets compensated through commission does not make them a dishonest salesman. Likewise, just because a financial advisor gets compensated through a flat-fee arrangement does not make them a saint.

3. You and your financial advisor should share similar values.

When it comes to planning for your family, your goals and values should be front and center, and factored into your planning. If you and the advisor have drastically differing life philosophies or values, then it probably won't be a great fit. I remember talking with a financial advisor several years ago who recommended I work full-time when the kids were little for the sake of accumulating wealth. He did not have children yet and could not understand why I felt I needed more hands-on time with my children over making more money. It is not that he was wrong or I was wrong— our personal values did not align. Therefore, we were not going to be a good fit. It's okay when you interview a financial advisor to ask them what role they think money should play in one's life, or how the financial decisions you will be making together will impact your personal goals and values.

4. Understand how your financial advisor chooses investments.

The investing chapter laid out various options for building wealth. All those options have unique strategies and benefits and some advisors may prefer one investment strategy over another. There's nothing wrong with that. It's important to understand *why* they think a certain investment is the best fit for you based on your unique situation, and if there are investments they like more than others or are adamantly opposed to. This will help you understand how their advice is influenced by their own unique filter, experiences, or expertise.

We had a client who asked us for a second opinion because a financial advisor recommended that she put a million dollars in an investment that had earned his other clients a 20 percent return the prior year. We encouraged her to find out if that was a one-time wonder or a proven strategy he has used over the years. It turned out to be the former and thus made it extremely risky for her, given her unique needs. Digging deeper on the financial advisor's own filter, experience, and expertise can help you make smart choices.

5. Your financial advisor should have a fiduciary duty to act in your best interest.

Not all financial advisors have a fiduciary duty to act in your best interest, although laws are changing more often now in the consumer's favor. Having a fiduciary duty means they must only recommend products or investments that are best for you, and not for any other reason, including the receipt of benefits to them over you.

6. Consider whether the financial advisor is a CFP (Certified Financial Planner).

A CFP designation means the financial advisor has completed additional training and education that has earned them the Certified Financial Planner credential indicating they are an expert in multiple areas of finance. This docs not necessarily mean that they are better at investing than other financial advisors who do not have this credential, but it does objectively indicate they passed a rigorous exam that tested their knowledge on various financial topics.

7. Find out the financial advisor's reputation.

Unlike other professions, it can be challenging to find public reviews of financial advisors, largely because their industry heavily regulates their online presence. But asking other professionals on your winning team for a recommendation or asking friends you trust who are a little further ahead of you financially can be a great starting point.

It is also important to understand what type of client the financial advisor tends to work with. A financial advisor who works with mega-millionaires may be appealing—they are great at making money for their well-heeled clients—but a financial advisor who is known for helping typical families make that leap may be a better fit. And the financial advisor helping your parents in their retirement years might not be the best fit for you if you're still in your wealth accumulation years.

Also know that it is okay to graduate from your financial advisor! A great financial advisor knows when you have outgrown their expertise or moved on to bigger levels. If they are not growing with you, do not be afraid to change.

THE CPA (CERTIFIED PUBLIC ACCOUNTANT)

Every winning team needs a S.T.A.R. CPA who helps you keep as much of your hard-earned money as possible within the parameters of the law. Too many of us parents rely on ourselves to understand the ins and outs of tax planning. Too many of us look to generic tax filing software or unsophisticated tax professionals instead of getting the right guidance! We may think we are saving money by not spending much for tax help, but we really are losing money by overpaying our taxes because we did not seek savvy tax advice.

My client who sells makeup through a direct marketing company recently bought an SUV. She had no idea the government would allow her to deduct the cost of her SUV as a business expense because it was primarily for business use and weighed more than 6,000 pounds. That deduction could significantly reduce her tax bill. When I asked her why her accountant did not tell her that, she said her husband files their tax returns through online software.

Working with a S.T.A.R. CPA can ensure you are maximizing your tax reduction strategies by getting the expert guidance you need. How many dollars have you left on the table by failing to work with a CPA? It's important to establish that relationship now! Here are some great tips for helping you find a S.T.A.R. CPA for your winning team:

1. Your S.T.A.R. CPA should provide tax planning services, not just tax filing services.

Establishing a relationship with a S.T.A.R. CPA should go far beyond filing a tax return once a year. You must work with a S.T.A.R. CPA who helps you strategize *before* you make any significant financial decisions, as this can significantly reduce your tax liability.

Before you max out your 401(k), sell your home, start a business, lease/buy a car, choose a certain investment strategy, or make any significant financial decision, consult with a tax professional who can help you understand the tax implications. If you wait to file a tax return once a year and then seek tax advice, it will be too late to go back in time and make difference choices.

2. Your S.T.A.R. CPA should know the ins and outs of taxes!

This should go without saying, right? But you would be surprised how many tax professionals do not have any background in accounting, or a professional license with the state. It's important to understand who you are working with and the extent of their expertise and training.

Generally speaking, accountants have a bachelor's degree in accounting, while CPAs have at least two years of accounting experience and have passed a rigorous examination through their state. If you are a business owner, you will also likely work with a bookkeeper who can help you keep track of your income and expenses.

Those chain tax-return centers don't necessarily hire only CPAs! Often, these mass tax-filing companies hire seasonal help and provide minimal training on how to file a basic tax return. And definitely be leery of having a friend or spouse without a professional accounting background do your taxes. While they can probably figure out how to fill out a form, they won't understand what tax strategies you should be using year-round or all the deductions you may qualify for.

3. Your S.T.A.R. CPA should focus on clients like you.

We all make money various ways. Some of us are W-2 employees, some of us own a business, some of us are investors, etc. If you own a doctor's office, you will want to work with a tax professional who works with physicians who own their own practice rather than a tax pro who serves W-2 employees. The former is going to understand the unique taxes, deductions, and credits that apply to you.

Likewise, if you are in a high tax bracket, you want to work with a tax professional who knows how to reduce your taxable income rather than someone who is used to working with people who don't make a lot of money. This is the best way to make sure nothing about your situation is novel to them, and that they have experience handling your unique issues.

4. Your S.T.A.R. CPA should mirror your comfort level.

Beyond qualifications and certifications, you need to understand your S.T.A.R. CPA's philosophy, meaning whether they are more aggressive or more conservative when it comes to using tax reduction strategies. Just like you have your own comfort level on investing, tax professionals all have their own comfort level on how aggressive they are willing to be when using the government's tax reduction exceptions.

There is a lot of gray area in the world of tax. Some tax professionals are less familiar with the government's exceptions to their tax rules or want to mitigate the risk of audit as much as possible. Other tax professionals can be extremely aggressive, and not all clients are comfortable with their more, let's say, "innovative" tax reduction techniques. Regardless of whether you work with a conservative or aggressive tax professional, make sure their approach feels right for you, and never, under any circumstance, allow your tax professional to engage in highly questionable techniques or use tax loopholes. Know that ultimately you will be held responsible for their actions on your behalf.

5. Your S.T.A.R. CPA must be comfortable talking with the IRS.

Even if your S.T.A.R. CPA files a legitimate tax return on your behalf, all of us are at risk of being subject to a tax audit by the IRS. That's when you are asked to provide additional information on the tax return filed on your behalf and defend the information you provided. A tax audit can be very stressful, which is why you should work with a tax professional who is very comfortable communicating with the IRS and can legitimately defend any and all deductions or claims made on your behalf.

THE ESTATE PLANNING ATTORNEY

Now we've made it to the best team player of all—the estate planning attorney! Okay, I'm only saying that because I am an estate planning attorney, but we usually are a big player on a family's winning team!

A S.T.A.R. estate planning attorney can help ensure that your assets and loved ones would be completely taken care of if you become incapacitated or pass away. In addition, an estate planning attorney can help make sure your personal, business, real estate, or other assets are protected from ill-intentioned third parties during your lifetime and after death. There's more! An estate planning attorney can provide tax reduction strategies using trusts, entities, or gifting. And beyond all that, a S.T.A.R. estate planning attorney is a trusted advisor you can turn to in your time of need and who can help ensure your entire team is working together in sync.

It's an incredible privilege to be an estate planning attorney and to be there for families during both their brightest and their darkest days. I am mindful of the great trust families place in us and am humbled by the remarkable resilience and triumph of the human spirit as I've personally watched families navigate through life's ups and downs. I believe I can speak for many other estate planning attorneys when I say that the well-being and protection of the families we serve weighs heavily on us and we don't take that responsibility lightly.

I want you to find a tight relationship with a S.T.A.R. estate planning attorney, one who provides you the invaluable legal guidance that you need, peace of mind knowing you and your loved ones are on the right track, and a feeling of safety and protection no matter what life may bring.

Here are some great tips to help you find a S.T.A.R. estate planning attorney:

1. Make sure your S.T.A.R. estate planning attorney primarily focuses on estate planning.

Estate planning is an extraordinarily complex area of law and should only be navigated from a licensed estate planning attorney who understands its nuances. Unfortunately, there are lawyers out there who try to practice multiple areas of law and dabble in estate planning, making it hard to develop an expertise in this field or keep up with the latest strategies or changes in law that will affect your family's estate plan.

You also want to make sure that your S.T.A.R. estate planning attorney can address the issues that are unique to your family. For example, a blended family may have different concerns or dynamics than a non-blended family, which requires gentle guidance and technical expertise. Or take a family who has a child with special needs, or an aging parent who needs daily care; those families will need expert advice and guidance from an estate planning lawyer who practices special needs planning. Wealthy families who will be subject to estate tax will need to work with a more advanced estate planning attorney with special tax planning skills and strategies. Make sure your S.T.A.R. estate planning attorney is trained in those specific areas that affect you and is honest about their level of expertise.

Furthermore, beware of paralegals or online legal drafting platforms that provide "do it yourself" generic legal forms that will

LAURA MEIER

likely not work for your family. Paralegal services and online legal drafting platforms come with very bold disclosures warning you to seek the advice of a licensed attorney and that they do not have any liability or fiduciary duty to you. You want to work with a licensed estate planning attorney who has a fiduciary duty to act in your best interest and can be held legally responsible if they make errors executing your plan.

2. Understand how your S.T.A.R. estate planning attorney will create your estate plan.

Every family is unique, but unfortunately, some attorneys use boilerplate forms and try to cram their clients into a one-size-fits-all document rather than one that reflects their unique needs and objectives. It's important to understand how your plan actually gets created and to avoid law firms that use copy-and-paste methods to create new documents for clients.

There are very sophisticated estate planning software platforms out there that estate planning attorneys can use to completely customize a plan for your family. These software platforms are extremely technical, requiring expertise to use. And they can create a beautiful plan in the end. They also get updated with the latest changes in law, so if your attorney has missed a small change in the tax code, they will likely get alerted. Ask your attorney how your plan will be drafted and whether they can verify that the plan contains the most recent changes in law.

3. Choose a S.T.A.R. estate planning attorney with a set process and ongoing service.

It's important to understand exactly what the relationship with your S.T.A.R. estate planning attorney will look like, starting at the

202

beginning with the steps you'll take together in setting up your estate plan. When will you make choices for your plan? What information must you provide? When can you expect to sign your final estate plan? How will your assets get connected to the plan? Who gets a copy of the plan? How can you make any future changes?

Get answers to all these questions before committing.

You want to work with a S.T.A.R. estate planning attorney who is service based, rather than document based. Attorneys who create estate plans and just send clients on their way are not providing their clients with the relationships they need to keep their plans updated. That is NOT the kind of estate planning attorney you can turn to in your time of need. Furthermore, you want to make sure your S.T.A.R. estate planning attorney has a great team in place so you're not always at the mercy of their availability. You also want to understand what happens to your plan if your S.T.A.R. estate planning attorney retires or changes law firms.

Another point on process and service: You want a S.T.A.R. estate planning attorney who understands how your tax planning and finances must intersect with your estate plan. For example, if your attorney is only focused on your estate plan, and does not seem interested in or concerned about assets or life insurance to carry out your wishes in your plan, then you know you are not getting the full level of service you need. You won't have a plan that will work properly in the end.

4. Understand how your S.T.A.R. estate planning attorney charges for their services.

No one likes a surprise bill, especially from a lawyer! It's important to understand up front how your S.T.A.R. estate planning attorney charges for services and what costs you can expect to pay.

Imagine this: You had a great visit with a prospective estate planning attorney, who took time to ask you questions and chat about your kids, only to get a bill for her hourly rate. If you knew she was charging $500 to talk about your son's preschool you would have skipped all that!

When you are setting up an estate plan, it's ideal to work with an attorney who charges a flat fee for the estate plan, meaning you will be charged that fixed amount regardless of the time involved. Setting up an estate plan involves many complex areas of your life, from who should raise your kids in your absence to how your name must appear on your deed for your home once you have a trust. Be sure that you can have all those conversations without fear of a larger bill. But fair warning, there are more advanced cases where it's hard to determine how much time is involved, which makes a flat-fee more difficult to establish.

The next step is understanding how you will be charged for any future access to the attorney once your plan is done. Can you call and ask questions or make changes without additional costs, or will you have to pay a new fee? Understanding the payment arrangement up front is the best way to start off any relationship and the only way for you to truly evaluate if the services you will be getting are worth the cost.

5. Your S.T.A.R. estate planning attorney should make you feel comfortable.

Estate planning is not strictly a financial transaction. A good family estate plan addresses multiple areas of your life and involves sensitive topics, ranging from your potential death to whether you want your step-child to inherit the same amount as your biological child, to how you feel about your family or friends raising your kids. It's important to have those conversations with a compassionate estate planning attorney who uses both head *and* heart when guiding you. You do not want a cold, technical experience where conversations about the well-being of your family are sidelined. The good news is that estate planning typically attracts attorneys who have a warm personality!

6. Your S.T.A.R. estate planning attorney should be highly reputable.

It's important to work with a S.T.A.R. estate planning attorney who has an outstanding reputation in the community, highly regarded by their colleagues for their expertise, work product, and ethics. While awards and recognitions can provide credibility, you also want to know how other clients like you have enjoyed their experience with that attorney. Fortunately, lawyers can be reviewed online through independent review sites. Take the time to read about other people's experiences with your prospective estate planning attorney. You can also ask other professionals on your winning team, like your financial advisor or CPA, or your friends who they recommend and why.

FORMING A RELATIONSHIP WITH YOUR WINNING TEAM

I hope you have a better idea now of who should be on your winning team and how to find them. The question becomes, who should you reach out to first?

The answer is in the 21-Day Family Nest Egg Plan in the next section of this book!

For those of you who wonder if it might be premature for you to be talking with these professionals, or you feel hesitant to reach out, please call their offices and talk with their staff. They will help you understand how they can help you or point you in the right direction if you both determine their services are not needed yet. Also ask if they have any helpful resources to help you become more educated. Lots of professionals have webinars and trainings you can attend for free online.

Don't forget that you are the captain of your winning team. I hope you now understand the roles your S.T.A.R. players will take on. But please remember that as their captain, you need to engage with them and make sure everyone's on the same page. Soon enough, their assists will have you scoring goal after goal. Don't forget, we parents are cheering you on!

A FINAL THOUGHT

As we wrap up the book and what I hope felt as close to "time together" as the written word can create, I am sitting at my kitchen table during the COVID-19 pandemic. My four kids are on zooms for distance learning, my high rise office is eerily vacant as my staff continues to work remotely, my home state is burning with wild-fires, my Facebook feed has blown up with political posts, and I am hoping my editor will be pleased with my work.

As we all occupy our seats in the arena of life, thinking about how to pursue our personal dreams, build wealth, and secure our family's future, while hoping to enjoy the journey along the way, I truly hope we can do so together by reaching out to the other faces in the stands with as much concern for their families' well-being as our own.

We all have an extra dollar, an extra hand, an extra minute, and some extra grace we can give to each other. If we see a family stumble—whether it is someone else's fault or their own—may we be among the first to help them up. Can you imagine how much further and faster we could go if we were truly in this journey together?

I know you will get those things on your **If Life Were Perfect** list. I know you will use your money for good. And I know you will help others on their journeys, too. Thank you so much for spending your reading time with me, and I do hope you feel like you can connect with me and my team at **www.thefamilynestegg.com.** I have tons of free resources to keep you moving forward. Cheers to you and a prosperous future. May God bless you and keep you always.

THE 21 DAY
FAMILY NEST EGG PLAN

ARE YOU READY TO JUMP-START start your journey to building wealth and securing your family's future? Our 21-Day Family Nest Egg Plan has all the basic steps you need to begin. And there's also guidance available at **www.thefamilynestegg.com**.

Day 1: Write your **If Life Were Perfect** List (page 14).

Day 2: Complete a Family Wealth Inventory Spreadsheet (visit www.thefamilynestegg.com).

Day 3: Determine your final payoff amount for each debt—credit cards, car payments, student loans, mortgage, and any other loans or legal obligations (page 22).

Day 4: Lock up your credit cards (page 36).

Day 5: Print your most recent banking and financial statements (page 21).

Day 6: Assign a grade next to your purchases and expenses (A being Superb, F being Awful) (page 23).

Day 7: Take the Day Off. Do not even think about your planning today. Turn your phone off and do something fun or meaningful with your family.

Day 8: Identify which expenses must be chopped or changed (page 24).

Day 9: Contact companies to cancel past service or to secure more affordable service (page 24).

Day 10: Prioritize which debt gets eliminated first with your extra money each month (page 24).

Day 11: Write down any expenses you want to ADD to your new budget.

Day 12: Identify five ways to increase your income within the next three months (page 35).

Day 13: Identify your next action step for each goal on your **If Life Were Perfect** List.

Day 14: Take the Day Off. Do not even think about your planning today. Turn your phone off and do something fun or meaningful with your family.

Day 15: Request life insurance quotes or have your existing insurance policies reviewed (www.thefamilynestegg.com).

Day 16: Schedule an appointment with a financial advisor (if you are in the black, not the red) (page 192).

Day 17: Complete the easy three-step process for naming guardians (page 159; www.thefamilynestegg.com).

Day 18: Schedule an appointment with an estate planning attorney to set up your estate plan (page 200. For Californians, visit meierfirm.com. I'd love to help you!).

Day 19: Schedule an appointment with a CPA for tax planning guidance (page 196).

Day 20: Donate or volunteer for something that does not benefit you (www.thefamilynestegg.com).

Day 21: Complete your family legacy interview (www.thefamilynestegg.com).

ACKNOWLEDGMENTS

THANK YOU SO MUCH TO my husband Josh for all your support. Thank you for loving me and being my partner and letting me talk out the book with you each step of the way. I love you and I am so proud of the life we have made together.

Thank you to my awesome kids, Conrad, Jack, Kate, and Andrew, for always checking in on me to see the latest word count and reminding me to research or call a friend when I was stuck. I see four incredibly special people when I look at you and thank God for you each day.

Thank you to my literary agent, Suzy Evans, and to everyone at the Sandra Dijkstra Literary Agency for recognizing the need families have for this guidance and finding a great home for this book. Suzy, you are an incredibly talented author and agent, plus anyone who golfs in ripped jeans with a PhD is a hero in my book!

Thank you to all those who contributed to this book, including David Leckey, CPA at Diversified Tax and Accounting; Kurt Beimfohr, Principal at Knightsbridge Wealth Management; Mark Seither, Partner at Kingsview Partners; Beatrice Schultz, CFP at Westface College Planning; and to all the families I've worked with through the years who have trusted me for guidance.

Special thanks to my dedicated team at the Meier Law Firm, especially Jonathan Johnson, Bonnie Johnson, Casey Wolff, Sydney Watt, Jessica Kiely, Esq., and Sara Leckey for all your hard work and support. May there be lots of celebrations together when the pandemic is over!

And finally, thank you to my editor Keith Wallman, Executive Editor and Editor in Chief, and everyone at Diversion Books for making this book possible. I am so grateful for the opportunity.

SOURCE NOTES

1. moneyunder30.com/compare-average-emergency-fund-savings#: ~:text=The%20report%2C%20based%20on%20telephone,have%20 no%20emergency%20savings%20whatsoever.

2. https://www.aarp.org/money/investing/info-2017/half-of-adults do-not-have-wills.html

3. https://www.bloombcrg.com/news/articles/2019-03-26/almost- half-of-older-americans-have-zero-in-retirement-savings#:~: text=The%20bad%20news%20is%20that,k)%20or%20other%20 individual%20account.&text=The%20Employee%20Benefit%20 Research%20Institute,out%20of%20money%20in%20retirement.

4. The Complex Story of American Debt, Pew Charitable Trusts, July 2015

5. https://wallethub.com/edu/cs/average-credit-scores/25578/#:~: text=The%20average%20credit%20score%20in%20the%20U.S.%20 is%20680%20based,%2Dto%2Dgood%20credit%20score.

6. https://www.cutoday.info/Fresh-Today/ Survey-Finds-It-Actually-Isn-t-Student-Debt-Weighing-Down- Millennials-It-s

7. https://www.experian.com/blogs/ask-experian/ is-it-better-to-cancel-unused-credit-cards-or-keep-them/

8. https://www.investopedia.com/articles/personal-finance/050214/ credit-vs-debit-cards-which-better.asp#:~:text=Credit%20cards%20 give%20you%20access,but%20they%20have%20lower%20fees.

SOURCE NOTES

9. https://www.lendingtree.com/auto/
gen-xers-carry-the-biggest-auto-loan-burden/

10. https://www.lendingtree.com/auto/
gen-xers-carry-the-biggest-auto-loan-burden/

11. https://www.autotrader.com/car-shopping/buying-car-how-long-
can-you-expect-car-last-240725#:~:text=In%20general%2C%20
however%2C%20people%20don%27t%20really%20keep%20their,
vehicle%20is%2071.4%20months%20--%20around%206%20years.

12. https://www.carsdirect.com/auto-loans/car-lease-term-short-or-
long#:~:text=A%20long%20term%20lease%20is%20considered%20
to%20be,average%20length%20of%20time%20for%20a%20car%20lease.

13. https://www.nerdwallet.com/blog/insurance/car-insurance-basics/
car-depreciation/

14. https://www.nitrocollege.com/research/
average-student-loan-debt#student-vs-credit-auto

15. https://www.nitrocollege.com/research/
average-student-loan-debt#student-vs-credit-auto

16. https://www.nitrocollege.com/research/average-student-loan-debt

17. https://www.creditdonkey.com/how-much-house-can-i-afford.html

18. https://www.fool.com/millionacres/real-estate-financing/
mortgages/4-reasons-avoid-30-year-mortgage-all-
costs/#:~:text=When%20Americans%20borrow%20money%20
with%20which%20to%20buy,but%20there%20are%20some%20
meaning%20drawbacks%2C%20as%20well.

19. https://money.usnews.com/investing/investing-101/
articles/2018-07-23/9-charts-showing-why-you-should-invest-today

20. hbr.org/2018/07/
research-the-average-age-of-a-successful-startup-founder-is-45

21. https://www.nytimes.com/2020/08/04/business/media/disney-earnings-coronavirus.html

22. https://www.forbes.com/sites/jrose/2018/12/13/how-to-invest-and-make-5-return-or-more/#77b311e01bd0

23. https://www.cnbc.com/2017/10/04/warren-buffett-says-this-one-investment-supersedes-all-others.html

24. https://www.forbes.com/sites/jrose/2018/12/13/how-to-invest-and-make-5-return-or-more/#77b311e01bd0

25. https://review42.com/what-percentage-of-startups-fail/#:~:text=An%20estimated%2090%25%20of%20new%20startups%20fail.&text=How%20many%20startups%20fail%20in,it%20to%20their%20fifth%20year.

26. https://www.cnbc.com/2020/06/16/billionaires-net-worth-grew-amid-covid-19-pandemic-from-market-lows.html

27. https://www.investopedia.com/articles/personal-finance/120815/4-most-common-reasons-small-business-fails.asp#:~:text=The%20most%20common%20reasons%20small,model%2C%20and%20unsuccessful%20marketing%20initiatives.

28. https://paymentdepot.com/blog/8-things-retailers-can-learn-costco-one-thing-not-follow/#:~:text=Costco%20has%20an%20astonishingly%20high,long%20term%2C%20especially%20hourly%20workers.&text=But%2C%20the%20price%20of%20employee,replace%20them%20when%20they%20leave.

29. https://www.cnbc.com/2018/08/09/millions-of-millennials-are-locked-out-of-homeownership-heres-why.html

30. https://www.usnews.com/education/best-colleges/paying-for-college/articles/what-you-need-to-know-about-college-tuition-

costs#:~:text=Among%20ranked%20National%20Universities%
2C%20the,News%20in%20an%20annual%20survey.

31. https://www.studentloanplanner.com/student-loan-debt-statistics-
average-student-loan-debt/#:~:text=Student%20Loan%20Debt%20
Statistics%20in%202020%3A%20A%20Look%20at%20The%20
Numbers&text=Borrowers%20in%20the%20U.S%20owe,to%20
the%20Department%20of%20Education.

32. https://www.allinahealth.org/healthysetgo/thrive/importance-of-
taking-vacation#:~:text=Health%20benefits%20of%20taking%20
a,more%20motivation%20to%20achieve%20goals.

33. https://www.nathab.com/blog/anticipation-is-the-happiest-part-
of-a-travel-journey/#:~:text=Looking%20ahead%20brings%20
more%20joy,happier%20than%20actually%20taking%20it.

34. https://www.cleverjourney.com/how-often-should-you-
travel/#:~:text=Ideally%2C%20you%20should%20take%20at,%2C%20
live%20happier%2C%20and%20longer.

35. https://blog.massmutual.com/post/interest-only-retirement

36. https://www.forbes.com/sites/
davidrae/2018/07/23/10-retirement-accounts-you-should-know-
about/#7a243afb2084

37. moneyunder30.com/compare-average-emergency-fund-
savings#:~:text=The%20report%2C%20based%20on%20
telephone,have%20no%20emergency%20savings%20whatsoever.

38. https://www.aarp.org/money/investing/info-2017/half-of-adults-
do-not-have-wills.html

INDEX

ABOUT THE AUTHOR

Laura Meier is a California family trust lawyer, podcast host, and business owner. She helps families secure their future by providing expert advice in career, finances, and family. Meier has spoken at Fortune 500 companies, and her work has been featured by national media outlets including NBC, ABC, CBS, FOX, Forbes, and more. She and her husband, Joshua Meier, Esq., own the Meier Law Firm (with offices in Newport Beach and the San Francisco Bay area), and they are the proud parents of four great kids.